BACH PERSPECTIVES

VOLUME 14

Bach and Mozart

BACH PERSPECTIVES

VOLUME 14

Bach and Mozart

Connections, Patterns, and Pathways

Edited by
Paul Corneilson

UNIVERSITY OF ILLINOIS PRESS
Urbana, Chicago, and Springfield

Library of Congress Cataloging-in-Publication Data
Names: Corneilson, Paul E. (Paul Edward), editor.
Title: Bach and Mozart: connections, patterns, and pathways /
edited by Paul Corneilson.
Description: Urbana: University of Illinois Press, 2022. | Series: Bach
perspectives; volume 14 | Includes bibliographical references and index.
Identifiers: LCCN 2022006732 (print) | LCCN 2022006733 (ebook) | ISBN
9780252044663 (cloth) | ISBN 9780252053689 (ebook)
Subjects: LCSH: Bach, Johann Sebastian, 1685–1750—Criticism and
interpretation. | Bach, Carl Philipp Emanuel, 1714–1788—Criticism
and interpretation. | Bach, Johann Christian, 1735–1782—Criticism and
interpretation. | Mozart, Leopold, 1719–1787—Criticism and interpretation.
| Mozart, Wolfgang Amadeus, 1756–1791—Criticism and interpretation.
| Walther, Johann Gottfried, 1684–1748—Criticism and interpretation. |
Music—18th century—History and criticism.
Classification: LCC ML410.B13 B125 2022 (print) | LCC ML410.B13 (ebook) |
DDC 780.92/2—dc23/eng/20220322
LC record available at https://lccn.loc.gov/2022006732
LC ebook record available at https://lccn.loc.gov/2022006733

CONTENTS

PREFACE

These papers were all delivered at a joint conference of the American Bach Society (ABS) and the Mozart Society of America held at Stanford University in mid-February 2020. We were fortunate to have an in-person conference less than a month before the world shut down due to the Covid-19 pandemic. The theme of the conference was the same as the title of this collection, which was Kathryn Libin's suggestion if I remember correctly. "Bach and Mozart" is a huge topic (covered admirably in a collection of essays by Robert L. Marshall, published in 2019), and the papers at Stanford spanned the eighteenth century into the early nineteenth century. The conference began with a panel discussion of Karol Berger's *Bach's Cycle, Mozart's Arrow: An Essay on the Origins of Musical Modernity* (Berkeley: University of California Press, 2007), which reminded us how musical aesthetics were fundamentally changing in the second half of the century. Although most people today think of Johann Sebastian Bach and Wolfgang Amadeus Mozart as the principal "Bach and Mozart," the conference, and likewise this collection, features contributions on the music of Johann Christian and Carl Philipp Emanuel Bach and Leopold Mozart, as well as their father and son, respectively.

The book is arranged more-or-less chronologically, beginning with Eleanor Selfridge-Field's discussion of the keyboard transcriptions of J. S. Bach and Johann Gottfried Walther, dating from the first two decades of the eighteenth century. Part of the impetus for arranging (mainly Italian) violin sonatas and concertos for organ or harpsichord was a practical matter for musicians who wanted to study and perform these works. But for Walther, who reportedly made more than seventy transcriptions for the keyboard (though most of these are now lost), this also seems to have been a compositional challenge to abridge, elaborate, or otherwise modify the models.

Yoel Greenberg offers a critique of the concept of "secondary development" in early sonata form focusing on sonatas by C. P. E. Bach and Leopold Mozart. He sorts out the different terminology employed by Charles Rosen, James Hepokoski and Warren Darcy, William E. Caplin, and Robert S. Winter, among other writers. While C. P. E. Bach and Leopold Mozart wrote famous treatises on playing the keyboard and the violin, they each came from different traditions (North versus South German) in terms of their composition. Nevertheless, Greenberg finds that neither of them (nor early sonatas by Wolfgang) represent the kind of "secondary development" that we find in the mature works of Haydn, Mozart, and Beethoven.

Noelle M. Heber compares the "pursuit of wealth" as it applied to the freelance endeavors of J. S. Bach and W. A. Mozart. Naturally, these two musicians had very different careers, with Bach living and working throughout his life in Thuringia and Saxony, while Mozart spent much of his childhood traveling from Salzburg to Italy, Vienna, Paris, and London. Although Bach was mostly employed by courts or city churches, he served as an impresario and conductor of municipal/private concerts and attempted to publish his own keyboard music (represented primarily by the series of *Clavierübungen* in the 1730s and 1740s). Mozart desired a court appointment away from Salzburg, but he had to make ends meet as a freelance performer, composer, and teacher in Vienna in the 1780s. (Had he lived longer, he would have been Kapellmeister at St. Stephen's Cathedral or he might have found work eventually elsewhere in Berlin or London.) Thus, these are two good case studies of the financial options for eighteenth-century musicians.

The next two essays focus on J. C. Bach. The first, by Stephen Roe, discusses his "German heritage," that is, his early musical training from his father and his half-brother C. P. E. Bach. J. C. Bach was only fifteen years old when Sebastian died in 1750, but the youngest son had already been pressed into service copying music and studying the keyboard works in his mother's musical notebook, the famous *Notenbüchlein für Anna Magdalena Bach*. From 1750 to 1755 he lived in Berlin with C. P. E. Bach and wrote his first six concertos and other works under his brother's tutelage. At the court of Frederick II, J. C. Bach was exposed to Italian opera and oratorio by Carl Heinrich Graun, and in 1755 Christian set off for Italy and began studying with Padre Martini in Bologna. And though J. C. Bach converted to Roman Catholicism and absorbed the Italianate *galant* style, he maintained his familial heritage even after settling ultimately in London.

David Schulenberg takes a different tack, comparing J. C. Bach to Mozart. Both composers discovered a mentor in Padre Martini, and the two of them met in London in 1764–65. (There is a charming anecdote about the young Mozart playing duets while sitting on Bach's lap and another about Mozart pointing out a pitch error in the print of Bach's *Zanaida*.) Not coincidentally, both became opera composers. (Mozart's "Marten aller Arten" in *Die Entführung aus dem Serail* is modeled on J. C. Bach's concertante aria "Infelice, invan m'affanno" in *La clemenza di Scipione*.) Schulenberg's conclusion might disappoint some, but he points the way to understanding their musical similarities.

The last essay by Michael Maul presents new documents on Mozart's visit to the Thomasschule in Leipzig in the spring of 1789. It has long been known that the choir performed one of J. S. Bach's motets, "Singet dem Herrn" (BWV 225), and presented him with a copy of the work. What was not known before now is the identity of one of the prefects whom Mozart talked to and apparently presented a (monetary) gift. Once again, Maul has been able to sniff out further evidence to supplement the report published by Friedrich Rochlitz. (It is worth emphasizing that Rochlitz himself was a Thomaner and likely was present at the time of Mozart's visit.)

Finally, I want to thank the other members of the program committee—Andrew Talle (chair), Kathryn Libin, Simon Keefe, and Ruth Tatlow—for helping to organize the conference. I also want to thank the editorial board of the ABS, especially Steve Zohn (chair), as well as all the people who served as readers for the essays submitted. David Schulenberg prepared the two indices. It has been my pleasure to work with the authors and Marilyn Campbell and Jennifer Argo at the University of Illinois Press.

Paul Corneilson, editor

ABBREVIATIONS

A	alto
A-Wgm	Vienna, Gesellschaft der Musikfreunde in Wien, Bibliothek
A-Wn	Vienna, Österreichische Nationalbibliothek
B	bass
B-Bc	Brussels, Conservatoire royal de Bruxelles, Bibliothèque
BDOK	Bach-Dokumente
	Vol. 1, *Schriftstücke von der Hand Johann Sebastian Bachs.* Edited by Werner Neumann and Hans-Joachim Schulze. Kassel: Bärenreiter, 1963.
	Vol. 2, *Fremdschriftliche und gedruckte Dokumente zur Lebensgeschichte Johann Sebastian Bachs, 1685–1750.* Edited by Werner Neumann and Hans-Joachim Schulze. Kassel: Bärenreiter, 1969.
	Vol. 3, *Dokumente zum Nachwirken Johann Sebastian Bachs, 1750–1800.* Edited by Hans-Joachim Schulze. Kassel: Bärenreiter, 1972.
BG	*Bach-Gesellschaft Ausgabe.* Johann Sebastian Bach's complete works. Edited by the Bach-Gesellschaft. 47 vols. Leipzig: Breitkopf & Härtel, 1851–99, 1926.
BJ	*Bach-Jahrbuch*
BWV	[*Bach-Werke-Verzeichnis*] *Thematisch-systematisches Verzeichnis der musikalischen Werke von Johann Sebastian Bach: Bach-Werke-Verzeichnis.* Rev. ed. by Wolfgang Schmieder. Wiesbaden: Breitkopf & Härtel, 1990.
CH-Zz	Zurich, Zentralbibliothek, Musikabteilung
CPEB:CW	*Carl Philipp Emanuel Bach: The Complete Works.* Los Altos, CA: Packard Humanities Institute, 2005–.
CWJCB	*The Collected Works of Johann Christian Bach.* Edited by Ernest Warburton et al. New York: Garland, 1984–99.
D-B	Berlin, Staatsbibliothek zu Berlin—Preußischer Kulturbesitz, Musikabteilung mit Mendelssohn-Archiv
D-Dl	Dresden, Sachsische Landesbibliothek, Staats und Universitätsbibliothek
D-DElsa	Dessau-Roßlau, Landesarchiv Sachsen-Anhalt - Abteilung, Dessau
DDT	Denkmäler der deutsche Tonkunst
D-F	Frankfurt am Main, Universitätsbibliothek, Johann Christian Senkkenberg, Abteilung Musik/Theater
D-DS	Darmstadt, Universitäts- und Landesbibliothek

D-LEb	Leipzig, Bach-Archiv
D-LÜh	Lübeck, Stadtbibliothek, Musikabteilung
D-ROu	Rostock, Universität Rostock: Universitätsbibliothek
D-SWl	Schwerin, Landesbibliothek Mecklenburg-Vorpommern
D-Tu	Tübingen, Universitätabibliothek der Eberhard Karls Universität
GB-Lbl	London, British Library
GB-Mp	Manchester, Henry Watson Music Library
GWV	Oswald Bill and Christoph Großpietsch, *Christoph Graupner: Thematisches Verzeichnis der musikalischen Werke: Graupner-Werke Verzeichnis.* Stuttgart: Carus, 2005–.
HWV	[*Händel-Werke-Verzeichnis*] Bernd Baselt, ed. *Händel-Handbuch: Thematisch-systematisches Verzeichnis der musikalischen Werke von Georg Friedrich Händel.* 4 vols. Kassel: Bärenreiter, 1978–86.
I-Bc	Bologna, Museo internazionale e biblioteca della musica di Bologna
I-Nc	Naples, Biblioteca del Conservatorio di Musica S. Pietro a Majella
I-Tn	Turin, Biblioteca nazionale universitaria
I-Vas	Venice, Archivio di Stato
I-Vnm	Venice, Biblioteca Nazionale Marciana
JAMS	*Journal of the American Musicological Society*
K	[Köchel catalog number] Ludwig von Köchel, *Chronologisch-thematisches Verzeichnis sämtlicher Tonwerke Wolfgang Amadé Mozarts; nebst Angabe der verlorengegangenen, angefangenen, von fremder Hand bearbeiteten, zweifelhaften und unterschobenen Kompositionen.* 6th ed. Edited by Franz Giegling, Alexander Weinmann, and Gerd Sievers. Wiesbaden: Breitkopf & Härtel, 1964.
KB	Kritischer Bericht (critical report) of the NBA
Lee	Douglas Lee, *Franz Benda (1709–1786): A Thematic Catalogue of His Works.* New York: Pendragon Press, 1984.
LMF	*The Letters of Mozart and His Family.* Translated and edited by Emily Anderson. 3rd ed. London: Macmillan, 1985.
LMV	Cliff Eisen, *Leopold-Mozart-Werkverzeichnis.* Augsburg: Wissner, 2010.
MBA	*Mozart: Briefe und Aufzeichnungen, Gesamtausgabe.* 8 vols. Edited by Wilhelm A. Bauer, Otto Erich Deutsch, Joseph Heinz Eibl, and Ulrich Konrad. Kassel: Bärenreiter, 1962–2005.
MDB	Otto Erich Deutsch. *Mozart: A Documentary Biography.* Translated by Eric Blom, Peter Branscombe, and Jeremy Noble. Stanford, CA: Stanford University Press, 1965.
MDL	Otto Erich Deutsch, *Mozart: Die Dokumente seines Lebens.* Kassel: Bärenreiter, 1961.

NBA   *[Neue Bach-Ausgabe] Johann Sebastian Bach: Neue Ausgabe sämtlicher Werke*. Edited by Johann-Sebastian-Bach-Institut, Göttingen, and the Bach-Archiv, Leipzig. Kassel: Bärenreiter; Leipzig: Deutscher Verlag für Musik, 1954–2010.

NBR   *The New Bach Reader: A Life of Johann Sebastian Bach in Letters and Documents*. Edited by Hans T. David and Arthur Mendel. Revised and enlarged by Christoph Wolff. New York: W. W. Norton, 1998.

NMA   *[Neue Mozart-Ausgabe] Wolfgang Amadeus Mozart: Neue Ausgabe sämtlicher Werke*. Edited by Internationalen Stiftung Mozarteum Salzburg. Kassel: Bärenreiter, 1955–2007.

NMD   Cliff Eisen, *New Mozart Documents: A Supplement to O. E. Deutsch's Documentary Biography*. Stanford, CA: Stanford University Press, 1991.

Passadore   Francesco Passadore, *Catalogo tematico delle composizioni di Giuseppe Torelli (1658–1709)*. Padua: I Solisti Veneti, 2007.

Rossi   Franco Rossi, *Catalogo tematico delle composizioni di Tomaso Albinoni*. Padua: I Solisti Veneti, 2002.

RISM   *Répertoire International des Sources Musicales* (International Inventory of Musical Sources). Kassel: Bärenreiter; Munich: G. Henle, 1960–.

RV   Peter Ryom, *Antonio Vivaldi: Thematisch-systematisches Verzeichnis seiner Werke*. Wiesbaden: Breitkopf & Härtel, 2007.

RV2   *Antonio Vivaldi: Thematisch-systematisches Verzeichnis seiner Werke*. Rev. ed. by Federico Sardelli. Wiesbaden: Breitkopf & Härtel, 2018.

S   soprano

SF   Eleanor Selfridge-Field, *The Music of Benedetto and Alessandro Marcello: A Thematic Catalogue with Commentary on the Composers, Repertory, and Sources*. Oxford: Clarendon Press, 1990.

S-L   Lund, Universitetsbiblioteket

S-Uu   Uppsala, Universitetsbibiotek

T   tenor

Talbot   Michael Talbot, *Albinoni: Leben und Werk*. Adliswil: Kunzelmann, 1980.

ThomDOK   *Dokumente zur Geschichte des Leipziger Thomaskantorats*. Vol. 2, *Vom Amtsantritt Johann Sebastian Bachs bis zum Beginn des 19. Jahrhunderts*. Edited by Andreas Glöckner. Leipzig: Evangelische Verlagsanstalt, 2018.

TWV   *Georg Philipp Telemann: Thematisch-Systematisches Verzeichnis seiner Werke*, vol. 3: *Instrumentalmusik*. Edited by Martin Ruhnke. Kassel: Bärenreiter, 1999.

US-AUS   Austin, University of Texas, Harry Ransom Center

US-NH   New Haven, Yale University, the Irving S. Gilmore Music Library

US-NYpm   New York, The Morgan Library & Museum
US-Wc   Washington, D.C., Library of Congress, Music Division
Warb   [Warburton catalog number] Ernest Warburton, *The Collected Works
           of Johann Christian Bach, 1735–1782*, vol. 48, pt. 1, *Thematic Catalogue*.
           New York: Garland, 1999.
Wq   [Wotquenne catalog number] Alfred Wotquenne, *Thematisches Ver-
           zeichnis der Werke von Carl Philipp Emanuel Bach*. Leipzig: Breitkopf &
           Härtel, 1905.

The Keyboard Transcriptions of J. S. Bach and J. G. Walther

Eleanor Selfridge-Field

During his Weimar years Johann Sebastian Bach was undoubtedly acquainted with his maternal second cousin, the organist Johann Gottfried Walther (1684–1748).[1] Both began making keyboard transcriptions early in their professional lives. For their initial efforts, both chose Italian instrumental pieces that were relatively new. Both conveyed a pioneer's knowledge of new approaches to genre, texture, and structural organization. Despite those similarities, a close comparison shows significant differences in detail and focus. Both composers' transcriptions come primarily from their tenures in Weimar. For Bach, in service to Duke Wilhelm Ernst, this limits the period under review from July 1708 to the early summer of 1717. Walther was the organist of Weimar's City Church of Sts. Peter and Paul (now the Herderkirche) from 1707 until his death.

Bach's original transcriptions do not survive. They are known through a core collection (bwv 972–987) in the Staatsbibliothek zu Berlin (D-B, Mus. ms. Bach P 280),[2] which was the source for the *Bach-Gesellschaft-Ausgabe*.[3] We do not know whether Bach transcribed most of the works in one concentrated effort or transcribed them over a few years. Walther's transcriptions, preserved in sequence in D-B, Mus. ms. 22541, are

1. My investigations of this topic, first aired at the joint meeting of the American Bach Society and Mozart Society of America at Stanford University in February 2020, have been kindly aided by Ray Heigemeir, Karl Heller, Jerry McBride, Laurent Pugin, Klaus Rettinghaus, Craig Stuart Sapp, Andrew Talle, Jennifer Ward, Steven Zohn, and Paul Corneilson. My interest originated in an extended discussion with Hans-Joachim Schulze many years ago. To all of them I extend my cordial thanks.

2. For details of further copies see Karl Heller, nba V/11 kb and images in Bach Digital (https://bachdigital.de).

3. bg, vol. 42: *Clavierwerke*, Band 5, ed. Ernst Naumann (Leipzig: Breitkopf & Härtel, 1894). This volume includes "XVI Konzerte nach verschiedenen Meistern" (bwv 972–987), hereafter referred to as bg XVI. The works are also published in nba V/xi.

presented as a curated collection in DDT, but they suggest a random collection.[4] The process by which German accretions found their way into both sets of transcriptions remains poorly understood, but some of its parameters are more fully documented than they were a generation ago.

In general Bach's keyboard transcriptions rely on concertos for violin, strings, and basso continuo as models, while Walther's emphasize concerti grossi. Bach's transcriptions follow their models more faithfully than Walther's. Many of Walther's pieces could have been transcribed a few years earlier than Bach's (that is, by 1710). Bach's original group skews slightly later (to around 1713). Walther's sources are variously Venetian, other Italian, French, and diffusely German.

Bach's transcriptions for organ are not closely considered here. BWV 593 and 596, based on Antonio Vivaldi's op. 3, nos. 8 and 11, differ from "keyboard" transcriptions in that they take advantage of Vivaldi's three-voice *concertino* (two violins and violoncello) to supply material for two manuals and a pedal (explicitly mentioned in BWV 593). This mechanism of textural transfer is not generally present in BG XVI (although Walther often employs it). BWV 594, based on Vivaldi's concerto for violin and strings nicknamed "Il Grosso Mogul" (RV 208), eventually appeared in print as op. 7, no. 11. It shares with BWV 592a and BWV 595 the use of concertos for solo violin and strings as models.[5] BWV 592 (for organ) and BWV 592a (for cembalo) honored concertos for violin and strings by Prince Johann Ernst.[6] BWV 1065 is based on Vivaldi's op. 3, no. 10, and is notable for its wholesale adaption of four solo violin parts to four solo harpsichord parts set against strings and continuo. Bach also borrowed themes for organ fugues from the Venetian composers Tomaso Albinoni (1671–1751), Arcangelo Corelli (1653–1713), and Giovanni Legrenzi (1626–90).[7]

---

4. *Johann Gottlieb Walther: Gesammelte Werke für Orgel*, ed. Max Seiffert, DDT, 1st ser., vols. 26–27 (Leipzig: Breitkopf & Härtel, 1906).

5. A recent summary of Bach's debts to Vivaldi can be found in Bernhard Billeter, *Bachs Klavier- und Orgelmusik: Aufführungspraxis. Beschreibung sämtlicher Werke eingeschlossen Kammermusik und Konzerte: Einordnung in Bachs kompositorische Entwicklung mit Anregungen zur Interpretation* (Winterthur: Amadeus, 2010), 377–91.

6. BWV 592 appears in D-B, Mus. ms. Bach P 280 as no. X (with the earlier VIII crossed out) but is excluded in the BG XVI; it is published in NBA IV/viii.

7. The fugues BWV 946, 949, 950, and 951 (951a) derive their themes from Albinoni, while the double fugue BWV 574 takes its subject(s) from Legrenzi's trio sonata op. 2, no. 11 (1655). See Robert Hill, "Die Herkunft von Bachs 'Thema Legrenzianum,'" *BJ* 72 (1986): 105–7. The "Fuga ò vero Thema Albinonium elaboratum et ad Clavicembalum applicatum" (BWV 923), sometimes attributed to Johann Pachelbel (1685–1764), is preserved in sixteen European manuscript sources. A theme from Corelli's op. 3, no. 4, is found in BWV 579.

The Culture of Musical Transcription

Multiple forces contributed to the rise of musical transcription in the central provinces of Germany at the beginning of the eighteenth century. One was the dearth of new music that resulted from the decline of music publishing in Italy shortly after 1700, despite a highly active two-century history. Another was the corresponding rise of the Huguenot refugee publisher Estienne Roger in Amsterdam, who found that his prints of Italian instrumental music found a bigger market than religious tracts and lexicons. A third was the growing practice of requiring serious music students to copy out scores to share with teachers and fellow students. Bach was a beneficiary and a preserver of unpublished music. For Walther, musical transcription was not an activity limited to his youth. He was still engaged in copying compositions by others for much of his life. Despite the latitude in his transcriptions, Walther is remembered today not only as an organist but also an incipient encyclopedist. His *Musicalisches Lexicon* (1732) has proved a useful resource for his knowledge of repertories of his time, although it also establishes the boundaries of that knowledge.

The rise of music editions in Amsterdam, chiefly those of Estienne Roger (c. 1665–1722), can be dated from around 1700, when he began to experiment with printing music. His first years as a music publisher were celebrated for quality and utility. The success of this new market led him in time to take more liberties with his prints, such that some were authorized by the composers themselves, while others consisted of Roger's culls from manuscripts in circulation. In Vivaldi's case, opuses 3, 4, 8, and 9 are considered to have been authorized but other opuses not so. We must therefore allow for a degree of nuance in interpreting what musical "matches" mean in these volatile repertories. After the death of Roger and his elder daughter Jeanne (also 1722), the business passed to Roger's younger daughter Françoise and her husband, Michel-Charles Le Cène (c. 1684–1743). Their enterprise lasted for two more decades.[8] Our interest here is predominately in the editions created under Roger's original imprint. Luigi Collarile's recent discovery that Roger may have been aided in starting his music-printing operation through an alliance with Giuseppe Sala (c. 1643–1727) in

---

8. The online catalog of the Roger firm by Rudolf Rasch, *The Music Publishing House of Estienne Roger and Michel-Charles Le Cène*, is the best starting point for tracing titles by the Roger-Le Cène establishment, https://roger.sites.uu.nl. Rasch notes the importance of François Lesure's *Bibliographie des éditions musicales publiées par Estienne Roger et Michel-Charles Le Cène* (Paris: Société Française de Musicologie, 1969). Lesure was able to date most prints up to 1716, but Rasch has painstakingly collated music print numbers with datable nonmusical publications to define outer limits of dates. See Rudolf Rasch, "Estienne Roger's Foreign Composers," in *Musicians' Mobilities and Music Migrations in Early Modern Europe: Biographical Patterns and Cultural Exchanges*, ed. Gesa zur Nieden and Berthold Over (Bielefeld: Transcript-Verlag, 2016), 295–309.

Venice and Marino Silvani (1644–1710) in Bologna is pregnant with possibilities that could have played a role in Walther's collecting activities.[9]

Because of the decline of music-printing in Italy, the practice of making handwritten copies to meet present needs had a revival that was evident in the smallest churches and the most remote courts. Large churches and monastic institutions often employed in-house copyists. Musicians' families (e.g., Vivaldi's father, two of his sisters, and two nephews) devoted many years of their lives to copying music. Freelance copyists eventually flourished. Yet across the breadth of this shadowy terrain we must be content with a paucity of detail.

Within central Germany Bach and Walther both culled copies, some provided by students, others used pedagogically.[10] Although Bach's music library (*Notenbibliothek*) now has a presence on Bach Digital, it appears that Walther, in common with Georg Philipp Telemann (1681–1767) and Christoph Graupner (1683–1760), was continuously searching for unfamiliar works in the libraries of his acquaintances.[11] In 1730 Walther traveled to Wolfenbüttel to make keyboard transcriptions from organ tablatures in the collection of Heinrich Bokemeyer, with whom he had recently begun a lengthy correspondence (1729–42).[12] Duchess Anna Amalia (1739–1807), princess and eventual regent of Saxe-Weimar-Eisenach, became a model of public access to literary, artistic, and musical expressions of the German Enlightenment, but the atmosphere in Bach's time was not so enlightened. Instrumental pieces by the Weimar court secretary

---

9. Luigi Collarile, "Estienne Roger, Marino Silvani, Giuseppe Sala: Prime ricognizioni intorno un'operazione editoriale complesso," in *Musicologia come pretesto: Scritti in memoria di Emilia Zanetti*, ed. Tiziana Affortinati (Rome: Istituto Italiano per la Storia della Musica, 2011), 103–18. Sala remained active until 1705. Some music was published from 1708 into the 1720s by Antonio Bortoli, who was mainly a book publisher. Collarile had recently compiled Paul Parstorffer's "Indice di tutte le Opere di Musica" (Munich, 1653), a reconstruction of the lost catalog of the Bavarian music publisher from which Walther gleaned many publication titles for his *Musicalisches Lexicon*. All but six of the catalog's 189 Italian listings cite prints from Venetian presses. See http://inventories.rism-ch.org/libraries/51006874.

10. Kirsten Beißwenger, "Erwerbsmethoden von Musikalien im frühen 18. Jahrhundert am Beispiel Johann Sebastian Bachs und Johann Gottfried Walthers," *Fontes Artis Musicae* 45 (1998): 237–49.

11. Also valuable is the commentary by Kirstin Beißwenger, *Johann Sebastian Bachs Notenbibliothek* (Kassel: Bärenreiter, 1992).

12. See Wilhelm Jerger, "Ein unbekannter Brief Johann Gottfried Walthers an Heinrich Bokemeyer," *Die Musikforschung* 7 (1954): 205–7; Harald Kümmerling, *Catalog der Sammlung Bokemeyer* (Kassel: Bärenreiter, 1970); *Johann Gottfried Walther: Briefe*, ed. Klaus Beckmann and Hans-Joachim Schulze (Leipzig: Deutscher Verlag für Musik, 1987); and *Zwischen Schütz und Bach: Georg Österreich und Heinrich Bokemeyer als Notensammler*, ed. Konrad Küstler (Stuttgart: Carus, 2015).

Johann Paul von Westhoff (1656–1705) and by Johann Ernst (1696–1715), the son of Duke Johann Ernst III (1664–1707), however, are preserved in her collection.[13]

Some copies of music traveled in the trunks of visitors and of diplomatic dispatches leaving Venice. Particularly during Carnival, those unable to be present personally sometimes asked for "souvenirs" from operas, typically arias and sinfonias. German visitors were especially prevalent in the years from 1708 to 1713. Among them we have been unable to confidently identify the "young prince of Eisenach" who arrived in Venice in December 1710.[14]

No one suggests that transcription was regarded as an art in its own right, but anyone who has reduced ensemble music for keyboard will acknowledge that in the process many musical choices must be made. Transcribers of Bach's time usually had practical aims. Libraries of transcriptions could have varied uses, including availability for study.[15] Access to sources of heterogeneous origin and quality might prevail over a single intended need. Transcriptions by pupils, pieces that were exchanged between friends, performing copies, and fair copies made for a single patron or library all existed in northern Germany. The identification of composers was not treated with the same significance as it is today, but currency in the musical language of the time was expected.

Transcriptions were made overwhelmingly by keyboard players, who were accustomed to integrating multiple voices into one coherent fabric. This process, then so appropriate to mundane needs, sometimes makes discovery of an original model today difficult. Bach is somewhat vague about instrumentation; the word *Clavier* could cover much ground. Walther is more specific in his terminology, designating all his transcriptions "appropriato all'organo." Yet neither in his chorale settings nor in his transcriptions does Walther consistently provide a pedal part, leaving performers to make their own choices.

Manuscript circulation as we view it here is only one part of the wider practice of "borrowing" that was prevalent at the time, as we know especially from Handel studies.

---

13. In the wake of the devasting 2004 fire in the Amalienbibliothek, musical access was reduced to microform copies and a catalog prepared by Angelika von Wilamowitz-Moellendorff; see https:// haab.weimar-klassik.de/Musikalienkatalog/.

14. I-Vnm, Cod. It. VI-485, 20 December 1710, fol. 2v: "È qui arrivato in questi giorni un giovane principe d'Eissenbach [Eisenach] della casa di Sassonia alloggiato in quest' albergo dello Scudo di Francia." Another German visitor of that season was Christian Ludwig, Prince of Mecklenburg-Schwerin; see Eleanor Selfridge-Field, *A New Chronology of Venetian Opera and Related Genres, 1650–1750* (Stanford, CA: Stanford University Press, 2007), 299–300.

15. Beißwenger, "Erwerbsmethoden," 240–42.

Types of borrowing were more diverse than we realize. Piotr Wilk shows that many concertos by Giuseppe Tartini (1692–1770) took their inspiration from Italian opera and cantata arias.[16] The energetic Bohemian Johann Adam (1678–1752), Count of Questenberg, assembled a lending library of recently composed works (often from Italy) in his Viennese townhouse, where he played chamber music with peers.[17] This means of expanding playing repertory in Thuringia was simply one species in a fertile musical garden.

Bach's Clavier Transcriptions

Bach's sixteen keyboard transcriptions are itemized, together with their models, in table 1.1. His core transcriptions consist of bwv 972–82, nos. 1–11. These eleven works are all preserved in the hand of Johann Bernhard Bach (1676–1749), and except in the case of no. 10, his version is considered primary.[18] Bernhard, a cousin of J. S. Bach, spent most of his life in Erfurt and Eisenach, where his tenure as a court cembalist overlapped Telemann's post as a court musician (1708–12). Bernhard and J. S. Bach were lifelong friends. Each was a godfather to one or more of the other's children. For Bach's no. 10, the copy in Walther's writing (D-B, Mus. ms. Bach P 801) is considered primary.[19]

The bg XVI transcriptions have long attracted interest because of the debts several of them owe to concertos by Vivaldi. At least seven works fall into this category. Of the seven known Vivaldi models, only three (bwv 972, 976, and 978), all from *L'Estro armónico*, op. 3, correspond to the versions found in Roger's original print of 1711. The latest addition to the Vivaldi roster is bwv 979, which is currently assigned to Vivaldi as rv 813.[20] Its alter ego (Passadore A.2.3.8) is attributed to Giuseppe Torelli (1658–1709) in S-L, Saml. Wenster Lit. D No. 28. The confusion issues from a set of part books external to both, in A-Wn, E.M. 143, cataloged under Vivaldi's name

---

16. Piotr Wilk, "Poetical Mottos in Tartini's Concertos: The Latest Concordances and Questions," *Musica Iagellonica* 9 (2018): 81–99, is the most recent in a series reporting these discoveries and their subtle relationships to their sources. Both in this respect and in their era (1700–30) they may share an attitude found in transcription networks in Germany. As in Germany, Vivaldi and B. Marcello provide some of the models.

17. Jana Perutková, *Der glorreiche Nahmen Adami: Johann Adam Graf von Questenberg (1678–1752) als Förderer der italienischen Oper in Mähren* (Vienna: Hollitzer, 2015). Several pertinent and parallel studies on this topic appear in Rasch, "Estienne Roger's Foreign Composers."

18. The group of twelve concertos includes bwv 592 (Bach's transcription of a string concerto by Prince Johann Ernst), which is also listed in the thematic index given on the final folio of D-B, Mus. ms. Bach P 280, but it is excluded in publications of the bg XVI.

19. Heller, nba V/11 kb, 99, notes Beißwenger's projected date of 1717 for the Walther copy.

20. In Peter Ryom, *Verzeichnis der Werke Antonio Vivaldis, Kleine Ausgabe* (Leipzig: Deutscher Verlag für Musik, 1974; rev. ed., 1977), it was listed as Anhang 10.

Table 1.1. Concordances for Bach's Keyboard Transcriptions (BWV 972–987)

Item No.	BWV	Bach's Key	Composer: model or analogue[1]	Cat. No.	Shelf mark in D-B, Mus. ms. Bach	Copyists[2]
1	972	D Major	Vivaldi, op. 3, no. 9	RV 230	P 280	JBB
					P 804	unknown
2	973	G Major	Vivaldi, op. 7, no. 2*	RV 299	P 280	JBB
					P 804	unknown
3	974	D Minor	A. Marcello, Oboe Concerto*	SF D935	P 280	JBB
					P 804	JPK
4	975	G Minor	Vivaldi, op. 4, no. 6*	RV 316	P 280	JBB
5	976	C Major	Vivaldi, op. 3, no. 12	RV 265	P 280	JBB
					P 804	JPK
6	977	C Major	B. Marcello?	SF A490?	P 280	JBB
					P 804	WNM
7	978	F Major	Vivaldi, op. 3, no. 5	RV 310	P 280	JBB
8	979	B Minor	Vivaldi, Violin Concerto*	RV 813	P 280	JBB
9	980	G Major	Vivaldi, op. 4, no. 1*	RV 381	P 280	JBB
10	981	C Minor	B. Marcello, op. 1, no. 2	SF C788	P 280	JBB
					P 801	JGW
11	982	B-flat Major	Johann Ernst, op. 1, no. 1*		P 280	JBB
12	983	G Minor	[Telemann?]*		P 804	WNM
13	984	C Major	[Johann Ernst?]*		P 804	JR
14	985	G Minor	Telemann, Violin concerto in G Minor*	TWV 51:g1	P 804	WNM
15	986	G Major	[Johann Ernst?]* [Telemann?]*		P 804	WNM
16	987	D Minor	Johann Ernst, op. 1, no. 4*		P 804	WNM

1. Items with asterisks identify titles for which a printed source appears not to have been the basis for Bach's transcription.

2. Sources given in Karl Heller, NBA V/11 KB (summary on p. 20) and in Bach Digital. JBB = Johann Bernhard Bach; JGW = Johann Gottfried Walther; JPK = Johann Philipp Kirnberger; JR = Johannes Ringk; WNM = Wolfgang Nicolaus Mey.

but including a violone part with "Torelli" written on it. The plot thickens with the observation that the sixth and final movement of RV 813 is also found in RV 522a, which is credited to Vivaldi only in a Schirmer edition of 1909.[21] This philology shows how tenuous many manuscript (and some print) attributions can be.

21. Peter Ryom, *Répertoire des oeuvres d'Antonio Vivaldi: Les compositions instrumentals* (Copenhagen: Engstrøm & Sødring, 1986), 110–11 and 234–35. Given the confusion, Heller, NBA V/11 KB, 90–94, remains a valuable anchor.

With respect to dating Bach's transcriptions, Hans-Joachim Schulze's studies of the 1970s and 1980s have worn well. In May 1713 Prince Johann Ernst was forced by deteriorating health to return from his studies in the Low Countries. Schulze deduced that the prince returned with some of Roger's recent publications of Italian music. Bach's access to this imagined trove would have been limited to the period between July 1713 and July 1714.[22] Schulze had earlier established that Bach's concerto transcriptions must date from "after 1713."[23] He had explored the question of whether Bach's transcriptions were arrangements only or commissioned works.[24] His *Studien zur Bach-Überlieferung im 18. Jahrhundert* evaluated more comprehensively the concerto transcriptions for organ and clavier.[25] He was now intent on pinning down which source Bach had used. This quest led to the discovery that Bach's transcriptions were not consistently based on prints. The content of Bach's arrangements of Vivaldi were shown to be from the printed op. 3, but those from op. 4 (*La Stravaganza*, 1716) and op. 7 (*Concerti a cinque strumenti*, 1716–17) must have relied on unpublished sources, for musical details in the German manuscripts differed and suggested earlier sources than the ones on which Roger's prints were based.

Tomasz Górny has now challenged Schulze's window for Bach's transcriptions in a documentary study of the firm of Adam Christoph Sellius, an agent of Estienne Roger in Halle and Leipzig. Vivadi's op. 3 was listed in Sellius's catalog supplement of 1711.[26] Górny suggests that most music used in the Weimar court in Bach's time came from the Halle enterprise, although neither of these two possible scenarios (Schulze's and Górny's) produce proof for one or the other. Górny's research on correspondence in the Amsterdam Stadsarchief, however, adds a new chapter to the complex picture of circulating music. He dates the collaboration between Roger and Sellius as one that began in 1709 and continued through 1716.[27]

22. Recent efforts to reimagine the path of these sources to Bach have included the possibility of their availability in Leipzig music shops by 1714, but arguments in favor of Schulze's scenario remain convincing.

23. Hans-Joachim Schulze, "Neue Ermittlungen zu Johann Sebastian Bachs Vivaldi-Bearbeitungen," in *Vivaldi Studien: Referate des 3. Dresdner Vivaldi-Colloquiums mit einem Katalog der Dresdner Vivaldi-Handschriften und Frühdrucke* (Dresden: Sächsische Landesbibliothek, 1981), 32–41.

24. Hans-Joachim Schulze, "Johann Sebastian Bachs Konzertbearbeitungen nach Vivaldi und anderen: Studien- oder Auftragswerke?" *Deutsches Jahrbuch für Musikwissenschaft* 18 (1973): 80–100.

25. Hans-Joachim Schulze, *Studien zur Bach-Überlieferung im 18. Jahrhundert* (Leipzig: Peters, 1984).

26. Tomasz Górny, "Estienne Roger and His Agent Adam Christoph Sellius: New Light on Italian and French Music in Bach's World," *Early Music* 47 (2019): 361–70 (esp. 362).

27. Górny, "Estienne Roger and His Agent Adam Christoph Sellius," 364.

Among the non-Vivaldi models found in the core Bach transcriptions, examples by the Marcello brothers, Alessandro (1669–1747) and Benedetto (1686–1739), are conspicuous. The relevant transcriptions are no. 3 (BWV 974), no. 6 (BWV 977), and no. 10 (BWV 981). Both men were highly active musically in Italy in the decade preceding 1715. The use of Alessandro Marcello's celebrated Oboe Concerto in D Minor (SF D935) in BWV 974 is not questioned, despite the fact that the version in C Minor in Schwerin (D-SWl, ms. 3530), attributed to J. S. Bach, still circulates. What is unclear is whether Bach encountered it in another circulating manuscript or as no. 2 in the lost Roger print no. 432 (1716).

Benedetto Marcello makes a secure appearance in BWV 981, where it is his violin concerto op 1, no. 2 (Venice, 1708; SF C788) that provides the basis for the transcription.[28] The part for *Violino principale* is missing in the Venetian Conservatory manuscript for op. 1, but fragments of it survive in D-B, Mus. ms. 13548.[29] Although Bernhard Bach copied this piece, Walther's manuscript in D-B, Mus. ms. Bach P 801, may be closer to the source.

Out of the nearly five hundred secular vocal works composed by Benedetto Marcello, few appeared in print. The exceptions were the madrigals op. 4 (Venice, 1717) and, almost a decade earlier, his two comic madrigals debating the merits of the castrato voice (Venice, 1708), which bore the printed title *Capricci*. In the first, "No' che lassù ne' cori" (SF A489), the singers (STTBB) deride the castrati, claiming they cannot enter Heaven. In the riposte "Si che laggiù nell'Erebo profondo" (SF A490), the castrati (SSAA) acknowledge the frivolous nature of what they are called on to sing and display their skills in chromaticism before launching into diminutions they claim to be able to sing for all eternity. (To underscore the point, this madrigal lacks a final cadence.) Dozens of manuscript copies of both pieces survive, most of them in Germany.

BWV 977 is not a true match for "Si che laggiù," but the similarity of rhythmic and melodic features reminds us how pervasive this configuration is throughout Marcello's repertory. It is found *inter alia* in his setting of Psalm 14 (Venice, 1724; SF B614).[30] In example 1.1 we see the opening melodies of BWV 977, an overture by George Frideric Handel, and the two Marcello pieces.

28. The subject of Marcello's second-movement fugue is echoed in Vivaldi's concerto op. 3, no. 11, which in turn was transcribed as BWV 596.

29. Similarly, the same part for the third movement of no. 4 (SF C789) and the first and second movements of no. 8 (SF C790) are found with it. Marcello's Sinfonia in A Major (SF C780b) is the first work in this manuscript.

30. "O Signor, chi sarà mai?" (SF B614) was circulated prior to publication by Marcello in order to solicit testimonials for his *L'estro poetico-armonico: parafrasi sopra li primi [e secondi] venticinque salmi di Davide*. The same opening is also found in Handel's Roman cantata *Clori, Tirsi, e Fileno* (HWV 96, 1707) but is not prevalent.

Example 1.1. Similar openings in (a) BWV 977; (b) the overture to Handel's *Clori, Tirsi, e Fileno* (1707; HWV 96); (c) Marcello's comic madrigal "Si che laggiù" (1708; SF A490); and (d) Marcello's setting of Psalm 14 (Venice, 1724; SF B614).

"Si che laggiù" may seem out of character for Bach, but the date and likelihood of its availability, in addition to its general popularity in Germany, are difficult factors to ignore. In combination they fall into the class of composers' "signatures" that are discussed periodically in digital musicology and music theory.[31] Properly, fingerprints recur over and over in the music of one composer but are rarely found in the works of others. In the absence of an exact match, should we pay attention to the occurrence of such fingerprints? This is a point on which historians and theorists often disagree. BWV 977 illustrates a fingerprint of sorts but one more specific to Venice than to Marcello.

The wrapper, labeled "Zwolf Concerte von Vivaldi. Für die Orgel eingerichtet von Johann Sebastian Bach" in D-B, Mus. ms. Bach P 280, is followed by a title page that reads "XII. Concerte di Vivaldi elabor[ato] di J. S. Bach" and signed by "J. E. Bach Leipsiensis 1739" in the lower right corner.[32] The normally accepted date for Bernhard Bach's copying is 1715. Approximate dates between 1727 and 1730 are sometimes given for subsequent numbers, with many later copies itemized by Heller and in Bach Digital.[33] Biographical dates for Wolfgang Nicolaus Mey (nos. 12, 14–16) are unknown, but he was an additional copyist of BWV 977 who seems to have moved in Telemann's orbit. Johannes Ringk (1717–78) copied no. 13. The later transcriptions

31. David Cope, "Signatures and Earmarks: Computer Recognition of Patterns in Music," in *Melodic Comparison: Concepts, Procedures, and Applications*, ed. Walter B. Hewlett and Eleanor Selfridge-Field, *Computing in Musicology* 11 (1998): 129–38.

32. Johann Ernst Bach (1722–77), the son of J. B. Bach the Elder, went to Leipzig in 1739 to continue his studies. The preceding wrapper, which is on later paper, is by Carl Friedrich Zelter.

33. See Heller, NBA V/11 KB, 119.

are based on examples that are largely, perhaps even entirely, German. Prince Johann Ernst and Telemann may be the only composers present, although attributions for bwv 984 (no. 13), and bwv 986 (no. 15) remain uncertain.

bwv 982 (no. 11), the last work in Bernhard Bach's hand, is a hinge between the two sections in that it is based on the first violin concerto in Prince Johann Ernst's later op. 1 (1718) but is linked to the earlier numbers through the continuity of the hand. bwv 987 (no. 16) is the fourth violin concerto from the prince's set. He is sometimes suggested as the composer of bwv 984 (no. 13), which is reminiscent of the widely circulated counterpoint exercises of Francesco Gasparini, a recognized authority in Italy and Germany and, until 1713, Vivaldi's superior at the Ospedale della Pietà in Venice.[34]

bwv 983 (no. 12), once claimed to resemble the sinfonia to *Herr Gott, der du uns hast von unsrer Jugend an* (twv 1:742), does not duplicate the content of the manuscript source in Brussels.[35] bwv 985 (no. 14) is considered to be based on Telemann's Violin Concerto, twv 51:g1. The third movement of bwv 986 (no. 15) resembles a Telemann aria,[36] although Heller finds the movement suggestive of Johann Ernst.[37] bwv 985 shows similarities to late instrumental pieces by Albinoni, especially his Concerto op. 10, no. 4 (c. 1735). The basic contours of its opening theme were familiar a century earlier in the bowed-string sonatas of Dario Castello (1621, 1629). The movements in Bach's transcription seem oddly unrelated in overall style causing one to wonder whether the work could be a pastiche.

Johann Ernst was tutored by Bach during his years as an organist in Weimar (1708–11). The prince had developed a keen liking for the violin and showed precocious skill in playing it. He could have observed the composer's interest in Vivaldi, which was apparently based on the melodic vivacity of Vivaldi's violin writing and on the rhythmic patterns and overall structure of his fast movements. Yet in orchestral works Bach would avoid adopting forms built exclusively on solo-tutti contrasts, preferring to interleave multiple soloists in such a way as to reserve the dominant role for the full ensemble. Given his age, the prince is unlikely to have had full command of virtuosic skills, although his posthumously published concertos show his attempts to master

34. The melodic shape strongly resembles three of Francesco Gasparini's two-part counterpoint examples in D-B, Mus. ms. 7105. Ten of Gasparini's years as the *maestro di coro* at the Ospedale della Pietà, Venice (1701–13), overlapped Vivaldi's tenure as *maestro di violino* (1703–15).

35. B-Bc, 941/68: *Herr Gott, der du uns hast von unsrer Jugend an* (tvwv 1:742), at https://telemann.omeka.net/exhibits/show/georg-philipp-teleman/les-unicas/b_bc-941-n--68. My thanks to Stephen Zohn for calling my attention to this source.

36. The aria "Herr, der starken Himmelsheere" from Telemann's *Liebe die von Himmel stammet*, tvwv 1:1044/3, employs a melodic contour similar to bwv 986/3.

37. Heller, nba V/11 kb, 131.

some of them. Vivaldi was fond of violin figuration in which arpeggios "hung" from a virtual "treble" anchored on the e" string (effectively the inversion of a pedal point), but for plucked and bowed instruments this meant rapid alternation between the high note and lower tones outlining a chord.[38]

Walther guided the prince's tuition in music theory during the last nine months of 1707. He heaped praise on his pupil in the dedication (dated 13 March 1708) of his *Praecepta der musikalischen Composition* (1708), which was written during the organist's first year at Weimar.[39] Walther assumed in the *Praecepta* a world generously endowed with violinists. He offered advice on articulation, word-painting, bariolage, phrasing, and other devices for improving the expressiveness of music. He addressed musical poetics, tuning systems, keys and clefs, consonance, dissonance, suspensions, four-part composition, imitation, modes, transposition, and various kinds of counterpoint.

The figure whose invisible presence connects the prince's music to both Bach and Walther appears to be Telemann, who never lived in Weimar but worked in Eisenach from 1708 to 1712. Bernhard Bach was his colleague there, and Telemann was godfather to C. P. E. Bach and to Walther's oldest son. Telemann also must have maintained a relationship with the prince during his time in Frankfurt (1712–21).[40] These two shared a common interest in the development of self-fashioned music-printing systems. The prince's objective, carried on into his last days near Bad Homburg, was to replicate his own concertos on a copperplate engraving. Telemann's efforts, begun soon after his marriage (1714), aimed at a simplified system for producing practical editions of sacred music.[41]

On 24 March 1715, less than five months before the prince's death on 1 August, Telemann dedicated his own (self-published) *Six Sonates à Violon seul, accompagné par le Clavessin* to the prince. The title page was undecorated, the style of musical typesetting French. No printer's insignia appears on the title page. No record of a personal

38. Luigi Ferdinando Tagliavini, "Interpretorische Probleme bei Johann Sebastian Bachs Orgel Transkription (BWV 594) des 'Gross-Mogul' Konzertes von Antonio Vivaldi (RV 208)," in *Orgel, Orgelmusik und Orgelspiel: Festschrift Michael Schneider zum 75. Geburtstag* (Kassel: Bärenreiter, 1985), 11–24, called attention to a passage of this kind in BWV 594, where Bach also used contrast between the Oberwerke and the Ruckspositiv to simulate Vivaldi's solo-tutti alternations. The adaptation of slow movements presented other challenges. The impressionistic Adagio was endowed with temperamental runs and clashing dissonances.

39. The two-volume treatise was edited by Peter Benary, and published in the *Jenaer Beiträge zur Musikforschung*, vol. 2 (Leipzig, 1955).

40. The prince's mother, Charlotte Dorothea Sophia of Hesse-Homburg, was the second wife of Duke Johann Ernst III.

41. Described in detail in Steven Zohn, "Telemann in the Marketplace: The Composer as Self-Publisher," *JAMS* 58 (2005): 275–356. Zohn's description of the decline of German music publishing brings a valuable perspective to the proliferation of manuscripts.

presentation exists, but such an event could have smoothed the path for Telemann to take custody of Johann Ernst's *Six Concerts: à un Violon concertant, deux Violons, une Taille, et Clavecin ou Basse de Viol,* published as the *Opera P[ri]ma./de ... Prince Jean Erneste, Duc de Saxe-Weimar: Par les soins de Mr. G. P. Telemann* in Leipzig and Halle, under the imprint of Kloss & Sellius (1718). The title page is decorated with a design entwining coats-of-arms, trumpets, timpani, violins, and recorders.

Telemann's *Avertissement* conveys the idea that he was among the eighteen-year-old prince's greatest admirers.

> To represent the extent and vivacity of his superior mind, I [cannot do better than to] offer you the beautiful moments of these concertos. [The prince's] life passed in only eighteen years. One must admire what he achieved in that time, especially in his understanding of the difficult art of music. . . . He mastered many instruments, above all the violin. The prince was attacked twenty-one months before his death [in May 1713] by a cruel and painful malady that eventually took his life. He never tired of composing; it was the best remedy for his illness. He did not have the pleasure of seeing the completion of this work before he died, but he made arrangements for its continuation . . . in a second volume that you will see shortly. [Oh,] that the Republic of Music may continue to hold in high regard his music and to honor the memory of this incomparable Prince! Not only did he delight us during his short life . . . but his works can bring us their felicities into perpetuity.[42]

The statement that "[the prince] made arrangements for its continuation" leads us to wonder what happened to the pieces intended for the prince's second volume. They are not among surviving manuscripts in Rostock, where copies of the first four of the prince's six published concertos are held,[43] nor are they in Weimar.

---

42. Abridged translation by the author of the *Avertissement* appearing in Telemann's edition of the prince's *Six Concerts* (1718): "Pour L'entenduë et le feu de son génie supérieur, on ne sauroit vous les bien dépeindre. Vous en trouverez de belles étincelles dans ales Concerts qu'on vous offre. Sa vie n'a passé que de peu diêxhuit ans. . . . Elle joüoit en Maitre de plusieurs instrumens, surtout du violon. Ce Prince fut attaqué vingt un mois avant sa mort de la cruelle et douloureuse maladie qui le mit dans le tombeau. Il ne laissa pas de composer; c'étoit là le meilleur remede dont il adoucissoit ses maux; Il entreprit même de faire graver cet Ouvrage; il n'eut pas le plaisir d'en voir la fin; la mort vint le ravir, après qu'il eut donné ses ordres pour le continuer, et y joindre une seconde Partie, que vous verrez dans peu. Que la République de Musique rende donc des hommages à toujours durables à la mémoire de cet incomparable Prince. On finit en disant que comme 'Empereur Tite étoit apellé durant sa vie les délices du genre-humain; de même aussi notre Seren.me Prince n'en a pas seulement fait les delices [*sic*] le peu de temps qu'il a vécu, par les belles qualités du corps et de l'esprit qu'il possedoit dans un degré éminent: mais que par ses Ouvrages il en sera même après la mort, les perpétuelle délices" (dated "Frankfurt le 1 febr: 1718"). No evidence of a second volume is known.

43. The four concertos are found in D-ROu, Mus.Saec.XVII:51:39a, 51:42(a), 61.7a, and 51:41. The first and third are attributed to Vivaldi (RV Anhang 12 and 11) in D-ROu, Mus.Saec.XVIII:61.7a and 7b.

Walther's Organ Transcriptions

In contrast to Bach, who sought out violin concertos as his transcription models, Walther was partial to trio textures, especially in concerti grossi. His interest happened to coincide with the peak years of that genre (1690–1710). He appreciated that any ensemble sonata involving two violins and basso continuo could provide the basis for a concerto grosso by selective doubling of certain passages. Walther showed that a reverse process, by which two violin parts could be transferred to organ manuals while the continuo migrated to the pedalboard, was equally viable. In practice Walther's transcriptions, like many of his chorale settings, vacillated between duo (manuals only) and trio (pedal added) presentations. The addition of the pedalboard could be a proxy for ripieno parts.

Walther's sources are more heterogeneous than Bach's and less consistently Italian. (See table 1.2 for a list of Walther's transcriptions.) They are also less closely observed than Bach's. Walther's aim was not (apparently) to replicate or enhance but instead to mine and recast musical ideas. The earliest print represented in his collection appeared in 1698. Where printed exemplars are known, they were available to Walther by 1708.

Walther's first two transcriptions are conventional and easily verified. Both come from the second book of Tomaso Albinoni's *Sinfonie e concerti a cinque, due violini, alto, tenore, violoncello, e basso ... opera seconda* (Venice: Sala, 1700). Walther's choices could have been based on Roger's print no. 7 (1702).[44] Both pieces evoke the celebratory spirit characteristic of Venetian string music at this time. Walther's third piece, offered as a "Concerto del Sig.r Blamr appropriato all'organo," which has long eluded identification, corresponds to an untitled six-movement suite for six instruments in a manuscript in D-ROu, Mus.Saec.XVII:51, which is preserved in the company of two works by Telemann. The mysterious Sig.r Blamr (an apparent misreading of Blamt.) proves to be François Collin de Blamont (1690–1760), a little-known but long-serving composer of court music at Versailles. His activity peaked in the 1720s, but Walther's source must have been earlier.

Walther's most familiar model (no. 4) comes from Corelli. The only sonata for violin and basso continuo (*violone e cimbalo*) used by Walther, his variations come from the opening *Preludio* of Corelli's op. 5, no. 11. Walther toyed with Corelli's initial material, ignoring subsequent movements. It is doubtful that he relied on a Roger print, for if he did, it would have been the publisher's no. 75 (1710), in which it is asserted that "purity has been re-established in its preparation,"[45] a point in which Walther clearly

---

44. Górny, "Estienne Roger and His Agent Adam Christoph Sellius," 366, cites Walther's Albinoni example, but the concerto numbers he uses do not correspond to mine, which come from Talbot.

45. Its loquacious title page reads that this is the "dernier èdition gravée proper à la joinder à ses autres ouvrages tre bien corregée tout nouvellement avec la gravée en partiture mais sans les agréements." This opus was widely circulated with all manner of ornamentation.

Table 1.2. Concordances for J. G. Walther's Organ Transcriptions (in D-B Mus. ms. 22541)

Item No.	Walther's Attribution[1]	Current attribution	Title of model (Catalog)	Print (City: publisher, date) or MS source (shelf mark)	key of model	key of Walther
1	Concerto del Sign.^r Tomaso Albinoni	Albinoni	*Concerto à 5*, op. 2, no. 8 (Talbot 2.8)	Venice: Sala, 1700; Amsterdam: Roger, no. 7, 1702[2]	G Major	F Major
2	Concerto del Sign.^r Tomaso Albinoni	Albinoni	*Concerto à 5*, op. 2, no. 10 (Talbot 2.10)	Venice: Sala, 1700; Amsterdam: Roger, no. 7, 1702	C Major	B-flat Major
3	Concerto del Sig.^r Blamr	François Collin de Blamont	[*Suite à 6*]	D-ROu, Mus. Saec. XVII:51[3]	A Major	A Major
4	Alcuni variationi sopr' un Basso Continuo del Sig.^r Corelli	Corelli	*Sonata a violino solo*, op. 5, no. 11: Preludio[4]	Rome: Author, 1700; Amsterdam: Roger, 1701 (no. 75); 1710 (no. 355)	E Major	E Major
5	Concerto del Sig.^r Gentili	Giorgio Gentili?			A Major	A Major
6	Concerto del Sig.^r Gregori	Giovanni Lorenzo Gregori	*Concerto grosso à piu strumenti*, op. 2, no. 3[5]	Lucca: Bartolomeo Gregori, 1698	B-flat Major	B-flat Major
7	Concerto del Sig.^r Manzia	Luigi Mancia	Sinfonia to the aria "Qui dove il fato rio lunghi"[6]	S-Uu, Inst. Mus. I hs 55:1	G Minor	G Minor
8	Concerto del Sig.^r Meck	Vivaldi	*Concerto a cinque*, no. 12 (RV 275; subsumes RV 430)	Amsterdam: Jeanne Roger (nos. 432, 433)[7] 1: A-Wn, E.M. 148.e. 2: S-L, Engelhart N. 90 3: CH-Zz, AM G XIII 1072 4: D-DS, Mus. ms. 441/1 (copied by Graupner, with obbligato flute) 5: D-DS, Mus. ms. 470/94 (GWV 918)	B Minor	E Minor
9	Concerto del Sig.^r Megck[8]	Vivaldi?	Concerto in D Major (Padua, 1712; RV 212)	1: I-Tn, Giordano 29, fols. 236–237; as RV 212, fols. 233–235 and 238–244 2: D-Dl, Mus.2389-O-74 (1716–17, copied by Pisendel, attributed to Vivaldi) 3: D-DS, Mus. ms. 411/21 (1745, GWV 318)	D Major C Major	G Major

Table 1.2. Continued

Item No.	Walther's Attribution[1]	Current attribution	Title of model (Catalog)	Print (City: publisher, date) or MS source (shelf mark)	key of model	key of Walther
10	Concerto del Sign.r Taglietti	Giulio Taglietti	Concerto op. 11, no. 2, movement 2	Amsterdam: Jeanne Roger (no. 422)	B-flat Major	B-flat Major
11	Concerto del Sign.r Telemann	Telemann	Concerto for oboe, violin, strings, and basso continuo TWV 52:c1 (1708–14)	D-DS, Mus.ms.1033/56a	C Minor	C Minor
12	Concerto del Sig. Torelli	Torelli	Concerto a 5, op. 8, no. 7, movement 1 (Passadore A.3:3.8)	1: Bologna: M. Silvani, 1709 2: A-Wn, E.M. 149 3: D-Dl, Mus.2035-O-5	D Minor	D Minor
13	Concerto del Sig.r Torelli	Torelli	Sonata for two violins (Passadore A.3.3.10)	D-Dl, Mus.2035-Q-1	D Major	B-flat Major
14	Concerto del Sig.r Torelli	Torelli	Concerto à 5, op. 8, no. 8 (Passadore A.3;3.2)	1: copy by Pisendel, in D-Dl, Mus. 2035-O-6 2: copy by Albinoni, in I-Nc, Rari 1.6/D. 20/1–3 (incomplete) 3: anonymous copy, C minor, I-Nc Rari 1.6/D	G Minor, E Minor, C Minor	A Minor

1. All attributions except no. 4 conclude with the words "appropriato all' Organo."

2. Title in Roger no. 7: *Sei sinfonie a 6, [sei] concerti à violino di concerto, due violini, alto viola, tenore viola, violoncello e basso continuo*. The numeration system was different in English editions.

3. Untitled, 6 movements, 6 instrumental parts (likely date: 1700–1710).

4. Walther discussed his "variations" on the bass of Corelli's opening bars in his letter to Heinrich Bokemeyer (6 February 1730).

5. Source identified in Max Seiffert's "Kritische Bemerkungen" in *Johann Gottlieb Walther: Gesammelte Werke für Orgel* (DDT, 1st ser., vols. 26–27, 1906), xxiii–xxxii. Confirmed by author in 2020.

6. The sinfonia is scored for two violins, two oboes, two bassoons, and basso continuo.

7. *Concerti a cinque con violini, Oboè, Violetta, Violoncello, e Basso Continuo, del signori G. Valentini, A. Vivaldi, T. Albinoni, F. M. Veracini, G. St. Martin, A. Marcello, G. Rampin, A. Predieri*. In book 1 (no. 432), the principal instrument is an oboe throughout, while in book 2 (no. 433), it is a violin. Concerto no. 2 in book 1 is "Alexandro" Marcello's Oboe Concerto in D Minor (the model for BWV 974). In book 2 (no. 433), nos. 8 and 12, in B-flat Major and E Minor, are attributed to Vivaldi.

8. The Roger firm's print nos. 486–487 (1721) contained Meck's *Concerti à 5*, op. 1, in which the final work (no. 12) was Taglietti's op. 8, no. 1.

Example 1.2. Opening of the Preludio in Corelli's Sonata for violin
and continuo op. 5, no. 11 (Rome, 1700).

Example 1.3. Opening of Walther's transcription of the same
Preludio (D-B, Mus. ms. 22541).

had no interest. Corelli's op. 5 fueled a century of competitions over methods of embellishment, but Walther used it to exhibit his variation technique, treating Corelli's
subject as if it were a chorale melody. Walther's modifications to Corelli's prelude in
no. 11 are shown in examples 1.2 and 1.3.

The sources for the next three works (nos. 5–7) are more obscure. Walther's no. 5,
a "Concerto del Sig.r Gentili appropriato all'organo," cannot be directly linked to a
surviving work by the Venetian violinist Giorgio Gentili (c. 1669–1737?). In a corpus of
six opuses (most missing one or more part books), no match for Walther's transcription
has been found in the five currently available.[46] Walther cited the *Concerti a quattro e
cinque*, op. 2 (1703) and op. 5 (1708) in his *Lexicon*. Roger reissued Gentili's *Sonate*, op.
1, and *Capricci da camera*, op. 3, in his prints no. 268 (1702) and no. 299 (1706). The
Concerti à quattro e cinque, op. 4, round out the list. The music-box-like opening theme

46. The five are op. 1 (1701): *Sonate à tre, due violini, violoncello, e basso continuo* (Roger no. 268); op.
4 (1707): same wording, with the continuo specification *violoncello o arcileuto con basso per l'organo*
(Bortoli, op. 4, 1707). Op. 2 (1703) and op. 5 (1708) are both entitled *Concerti a quattro e cinque*; op.
3 (1708) is entitled *Capricci: XII sonate à violino e violoncello* (incomplete unicum in I-Vc damaged in
flood of 12 November 2019); op. 6 (1716) known only from the presentation copy *Concerti a quattro*,
dedicated to Friedrich August, Prince of Saxony, probably made for the prince's visit to Venice in
1716–17, in D-Dl, Mus.2164-O-1.

of Walther's transcription is not characteristic of Gentili, who emphasized repeated-note sequences and arpeggiated figures. A rough analogue to the opening melody of no. 5 can be found, however, in numerous eighteenth-century manuscript copies of an anonymous *balletto*.[47]

Walther's no. 6 comes from a concerto grosso by the violinist Giovanni Lorenzo Gregori (1663–1745), who was little known outside his native Lucca. Gregori's music is notable for its fluid treatment of genre, not only in the ten *Concerti grossi à più strumenti*, op. 2 (from which no. 3 is Walther's no. 6), but also in his thirty-six *Arie in stile francese a 1 e 2 voci*, which take the form of minuets, bourrées, and galliards. Both publications were issued in Lucca in 1698 by Bartolomeo Gregori.

Luigi Mancia (c. 1665–1708) created the model for Walther's no. 7, but it is not known how Walther became acquainted with it. Mancia's source is preserved today only as the sinfonia to a vocal work, "Qui dove il fatto rio lungo," in S-Uu, Inst. Mus. I hs 55:1. Born in Brescia, Mancia moved between Germany and Italy at intervals. After an apprenticeship in Hanover (1680s), he resettled in Rome (1690s). His last-known appearances were in Venice (1706–8), where German ties were still evident: his setting of the opera *Alessandro in Susa* (San Giovanni Grisostomo, 28 January 1708) was dedicated to Karl Alexander, Duke of Wittenberg.[48]

Walther leads us astray in nos. 8 and 9 with attributions to Joseph Meck (1690–1758), a Bavarian composer who studied in Italy from around 1708 to 1711, then joined the court in Eichstätt as a violinist in 1712 and remained there all his life, serving as kapellmeister from 1720. But these two transcriptions are not based on Meck's compositions.[49] Nos. 8 and 9 derive principally from Vivaldi, who has not previously been associated with Walther. Neither lineage is straightforward, partly because Graupner was involved in the transmission chain. The sometimes porous boundary between Graupner and Vivaldi can be difficult to delineate. Graupner was an impeccable copyist with a penchant for adding wind and brass parts to the works he copied. (In these endeavors his work ran parallel to Johann Pisendel's in Dresden, for the Saxon was prone to add oboe parts to Italian string concertos.) Both Graupner and Vivaldi en-

---

47. See D-Tu, Balletto, anonymous, Mk 12 [RISM ID: 455017974] and D-LÜh, Mus. N 1861a [RISM ID: 452012382]. Roughly a dozen loosely analogous examples can be found elsewhere in the RISM OPAC.

48. The music is attributed to Mancia, the libretto to Roberto Frigimelica-Roberti. The electress of Bavaria, Theresa Kunegunda Sobieska, was probably present at the opening performance. For context and details, see Selfridge-Field, *A New Chronology*, 283–84.

49. Jeanne Roger published Meck's *Concerti grossi* op. 1 (nos. 486–87) in 1721. Citing Robert Eitner's *Quellenlexikon* as its source, RISM (2020) gives Meck as the composer. Klaus Beckmann, *Joseph Meck (1690–1758): Leben und Werk des Eichstaetter Hofkapellmeisters* (Bochum: Rohr Universität, 1975), offers background.

joyed the patronage of the landgraves of Hesse-Darmstadt: Graupner (from 1709) as kapellmeister to the elder landgrave Ernst Ludwig (1667–1739) and Vivaldi (officially 1718–20 but informally for a much longer time) as *maestro di camera* to Landgrave Philipp (1671–1736). Philipp was dispatched to Mantua as imperial governor after the collapse of the Gonzaga duchy. Several singers who appeared at Sant'Angelo, where Vivaldi was active intermittently for years, secured long-term patronage from German noblemen in the 1710s. Vivaldi remained in close touch with Prince Philipp, who made periodic trips to Venice, until the nobleman's death.

Walther's no. 8 is credited to Vivaldi (as RV 275) in Jeanne Roger's print no. 433. Among four manuscript copies it is attributed to Vivaldi in three and to Graupner in one (as GWV 918; RV 275a). This transcription reminds us of the caveat that some Roger anthologies were publishers' miscellanies and direct proof of authorship in cases like this one is ultimately lacking. In no. 9 the second and third movements correspond to the first two in Vivaldi's concerto for "La Festa della Lingua di Sant'Antonio" (RV 212), which was composed for the eponymous feast in the 1712 at Padua's cathedral. The source of Walther's short introductory movement is unknown. It could be an improvisation of his own.[50] Pisendel's copy in C major (attributed to Vivaldi in D-Dl, Mus.2389-O-74) was made in 1716 or 1717. Its elaborate cadenzas do not appear in Walther's transcription. A different slow movement appears in the Turin autograph, in which some ripieno parts are omitted.[51] The Darmstadt source (D-DS, Mus. ms. 411/21), with added flute (credited to Graupner as GWV 318), is dated 1745 and similarly cannot have been Walther's model.

Walther's alphabetical ordering becomes clear in the last five transcriptions (nos. 10–14), said to be by Taglietti, Telemann, and Torelli. The Brescian priest Giulio Taglietti (c. 1660–1718) was a violin teacher and a composer at the Jesuit College in his native city. No. 10 utilizes the second movement of his Concerto op. 11, no. 2. Walther could have encountered the model in Roger's reprint no. 422 (*Concerti a quattro con i suoi rinforzi*, c. 1717), but because his transcription deviates substantially from the print, it seems likely that he worked from a manuscript or freely invented some of the content.

Like Bach and Graupner, Telemann had received a classical education. While still in Magdeburg, he became a proficient player of violin, transverse flute, and keyboard, and learned to play additional instruments in adolescence. In his entry for Telemann in the *Musicalisches Lexicon*, Walther stressed the diversity of Telemann's works, his

50. The third movement finds its closest match in an anonymous English piece, Finney MS 41, in US-AUS [RISM ID: 1000115572].

51. Walther cannot have seen the Turin source, which resided in the home of Vivaldi's unwed sisters into the 1760s.

contributions to pedagogy, his portfolio of evangelical pieces, and his multiple appointments in Hamburg. Walther's no. 11 leads a curious path to a firm identity. Its model is ostensibly Telemann's Oboe Concerto in C Minor, TWV 52:c1. Its four movements as given by Walther correspond to the surviving parts in Lund (S-L, Saml. Engelhart No. 370), which are attributed to "Wivald" [Vivaldi]. In his provisional catalog of 1974 Peter Ryom rejected the Vivaldi attribution, and the work retains its position as Anh. 17 in RV2.[52] While there is nothing distinctively Vivaldian about the music, the absence of an early Telemann source should be noted. Another entanglement between Telemann and Vivaldi occurs in a "Concerto per la Chiesa" transcribed by Walther,[53] but here Telemann's authorship is not confirmed; the music matches an anonymous aria, "Erleuchte mich, du wahres Licht" (TWV 33: Anh. 2).

Walther's last three transcriptions (nos. 12–14) come from late works by Torelli.[54] Relative to his other transcriptions, the sources are easily verified. No. 12 corresponds to Torelli's op. 8, no. 7 (Passadore A.3.2.8).[55] Nos. 13 and 14 (Passadore A.3.3.10 and A.2.3.2) are based on D-Dl, Mus. 2035-Q-1 and Mus. 2035-O-6. The latter, found in the hand of Pisendel in D-Dl, is also found in Albinoni's incomplete copy in I-Nc, Rari 1.6/D.20/1–3.

Walther's tendency to deviate in both text and musical content is not news but it is nonetheless striking. Apart from his study of Bach's debts (in BWV 594) to Vivaldi's "Grosso Mogul" Concerto (RV 208), which found its way into print as op. 7, no. 11,[56] Luigi Ferdinando Tagliavini emphasized the independence of Walther's transcriptions of Albinoni (in nos. 1 and 2) and Gregori (in no. 6).[57] Walther's treatment of Corelli and Taglietti merits a similar verdict.

52. Ryom, *Verzeichnis der Werke Antonio Vivaldis, Kleine Ausgabe*, 139. Ryom retains the attribution on the basis of its inclusion under Telemann's name in the first supplement to *The Breitkopf Thematic Catalogue: The Six Parts and Sixteen Supplements, 1762–1787*, ed. Barry S. Brook (New York: Dover, 1966).

53. US-NH, Ma21.Y11.T23 (LM 4794). A later copy was made by Rincks's son, Johann Christian Heinrich (1770–1846).

54. Walther's admiration for Torelli is expressed in the two columns he accorded him in the *Musicalisches Lexicon*. He reported his admission to the Academia Filarmonica, Bologna, his position as a violinist at San Petronio, and his appointment as concertmaster in Ansbach (in "1703," although the actual date was earlier). Walther also praised the varied instrumentation and textures of Torelli's instrumental works.

55. From the "Concerti grossi con pastorale per il santissimo Natale" (Bologna, 1709). Three of the performing parts for this work in A-Wn, E.M. 149, are attributed to Vivaldi.

56. As RV 208a, signifying a variant second movement.

57. Luigi Ferdinando Tagliavini, "Johann Gottfried Walther trascrittore," *Analecta Musicologica* 7 (1969): 112–19.

Bach, in contrast, was a careful examiner and an attentive transcriber. He might enhance or adapt but he did not violate the integrity of preexisting material as nonchalantly as Walther did. Where Walther abridged, interpolated, elaborated, or omitted, Bach's modifications were musically motivated. In his organ adaptations of Vivaldi, Bach necessarily modified the upper register to suit the Weimar organ, which did not reach beyond c'''. Bach increased the activity in inner voices to create virtual textures of four or more voices within the scope of one actual instrument. Walther demonstrated the same tendency when adapting works that were originally for solo voice, such as Corelli's Sonata op. 5, no. 11. Both continuously projected a sense of constant, metered motion in fast and moderate tempos. Bach selectively "completed" some of Vivaldi's harmonies, especially where the Italian was inclined to emphasize treble and bass while ignoring interior voices. (In later years Vivaldi often failed to fill in viola parts in his manuscripts.)

Many accounts note the extent to which Bach's use of the ritornello evolved in both his instrumental works and his cantata sinfonias. Such currents are evident in thematic extensions and the structures they sometimes impose. Yet Bach did not seek to imitate the block structure of early concerto allegro movements: he did not strictly segregate soloists from ripienists with the same rigor as many Italians did. He also did not scaffold timbres by piling them up to increase volume. Bach's Brandenburgs and especially his orchestral suites usually employ an integral approach rotating from one soloist to the next.

Mood may also figure in a comparison between Bach and his models. Vivaldi's cheerful demeanor should have brought a sense of relief to the often gloomy world of Lutheran church music. Many commentators cite Bach's interest in injecting a sense of spiritual joy into his music, and it is fair to allow that this was spontaneous, but Vivaldi offered novel ways in which Bach might achieve balance in his repertory. Cesare Fertonani detects a clash between mood and message in Bach's quotation of "La Primavera" (op. 8, no. 1) in BWV 27, *Wir weiß, wie nahe mir mein Ende*.[58] A broader enquiry awaits investigation.

We know that Walther valued Bach's transcriptions highly, although the possible role that Prince Johann Ernst played is unknown. In a letter to Bokemeyer (September 1740) the composer reported his decision to sell his transcriptions, which he regarded as "his most cherished possession," because of financial need, and in his autobiographical notes prepared for Johann Mattheson's *Grundlage einer Ehren-Pforte*, Walther mentioned transcribing seventy-eight instrumental works for keyboard.[59] The

---

58. Cesare Fertonani, "Ancora su Vivaldi e Bach," in *"Fulgeat sol frontis decorae": Studi in onore di Michael Talbot* (Venezia: Fondazione Giorgio Cini, 2016), 115–28.

59. In *Grundlage einer Erhen-Pforte* (Hamburg, 1740), 389. Walther's list of works concludes: "von mir aufs Clavier applicirte Stücke, 78 an der Zahl."

number matches that linked to an earlier claim by the prince to possess a collection of seventy-eight keyboard transcriptions.[60] Were the collections one and the same? Walther could have transcribed some of these works for the prince prior to the latter's journey to Utrecht, but he could also have transcribed more after the prince's return.

Finally, we must note that keyboard transcriptions of Bach and Walther's era floated on a broad tide of adaptation and allusion that swelled periodically from their time to ours. In the case of Vivaldi's op. 3, for example, nos. 5, 7, 9, and 12 were transcribed for clavichord by an otherwise unknown Englishwoman, Anne Dawson.[61] Perhaps working from Walsh reprints, she also adapted eight concertos from Vivaldi's op. 4 and pieces by other (mainly Italian) contemporaries.[62] By comparison to both Bach's and Walther's efforts her textures are thinner and an impression of perpetual motion absent, but a thickening of the bass register (often with doubled octaves) is conspicuous. French transcriptions and arrangements of both concertos and sonatas by Vivaldi were imaginatively refashioned as everything from pastoral suites with optional hurdy-gurdy to *grands motets*. Quotations from Marcello's works were in subsequent generations threaded through sacred vocal music in England, counterpoint exercises in France, and grand opera in Italy but rarely, if ever, used in keyboard music. In contrast, Bach and Walther shared similar conceptualizations of their tasks, even when their works were elaborated differently. Neither composer trivialized nor aggrandized his models. They simply embedded them in idioms familiar to their immediate listeners.

60. Billeter, *Bachs Klavier- und Orgelmusik*, 377: "Johann Ernst habe 78 Concerti aufs Clavier applicirt" (no source given).

61. See GB-Mp, Rm710.5Cr71. The four Dawson transcriptions from Vivaldi's op. 3 are hyperlinked to http://vivaldi-op3.ccarh.org.

62. Her heavily ornamented renderings of op. 4, nos. 1 and 6 find rough parallels in BWV 980 and BWV 975.

Precedents for the "Secondary Development" from Bach to Mozart and Their Implications for Understanding Early Sonata Form

Yoel Greenberg

Introduction

When Alexandre Oulibicheff spoke of the "propensity to relapse into chaos" in the finale of Mozart's "Jupiter Symphony," there can be little doubt of at least one passage he had in mind.[1] Only eight measures after the onset of the recapitulation, the orchestra erupts, bellowing out the main theme in relentlessly rising sequence above brusque slides in the lower strings and beneath a chromatic, fourth-species-style counterpoint, spread over three octaves in the winds. In the midst of the third iteration of the theme, all havoc breaks loose. The violins cross swords in stretto above a distorted version of the theme in the bass, as the sequence descends back down amid rising chromatic screeches in the winds. Then all at once, chaos is banished, and the festivities of the exposition resume.

We do not usually expect such extreme drama at this stage in sonata form. The recapitulation is associated with reestablishing a sense of equilibrium and homecoming, whereas the high points of the drama usually occur in the development or, as in many works by Beethoven or the same movement by Mozart, in the coda. Appearing at this point, Mozart's horror-movie sequence, or his "dissonant passage" as Elaine Sisman named it—an understatement if there ever was one—appears to defy reason.

1. Alexandre Oulibicheff, "The 'Jupiter' Symphony of Mozart," *Dwight's Journal of Music* 27, no. 16 (1867): 121–22; reprinted in Elaine R. Sisman, *Mozart: The "Jupiter" Symphony* (Cambridge: Cambridge University Press, 1993), 80–85. This research was supported by the Israel Science Foundation (grant no. 1929/18).

23

As Sisman aptly puts it, "the theme goes up and down in an unmotivated sequence which calls into question every possible meaning that the theme has previously suggested . . . disordered and obscure, massive and repetitious."[2] By the time it is over, we have almost forgotten the little repeat of the main theme in the tonic and return to the material of the exposition's transition with a sense of relief.

Mozart's dissonant passage is an extreme example of a phenomenon widely commented upon by scholars of sonata form, whereby an unstable episode appears within the confines of the recapitulation, either in the area of the primary theme or within the transition. Charles Rosen called such passages "Secondary Development sections":

> The Secondary Development section appears in the great majority of late eighteenth-century works soon after the beginning of the recapitulation and often with the second phrase. Sometimes it is only a few bars long, sometimes very extensive indeed. The purpose of this section is to lower harmonic tension without sacrificing interest; it introduces an allusion to the subdominant or to the related "flat" keys.[3]

Rosen goes on to say, "It would be a mistake to identify the appearance of the subdominant with the necessary tonal alteration of harmony to transform an exposition that goes from tonic to dominant into a recapitulation that remains in the tonic." He cites as evidence that "the Secondary Development as often as not returns to one of the themes of the first group, which necessitates a still further change later in the section in order to bring the second group into the tonic."[4]

James Hepokoski and Warren Darcy's entire discussion of the recapitulation of the transition in *Elements of Sonata Theory* is framed as a critique of Rosen's stance, which they view as "overstated and asserted in the abstract," claiming that Rosen's example of a nonfunctional flat-side tilt, the first movement of Beethoven's "Waldstein Sonata," is "a snapshot from the late and much-developed stage in the history of the 'classical' sonata."[5] In Hepokoski and Darcy's view, the feint to the subdominant was originally motivated by harmonic considerations, but then became a "quick fix" after 1780, providing composers "an opportunity to generate 'false' or 'surplus' flat-side leaning passages" that were "functionally superfluous."[6]

In this chapter I will bring evidence from mid-eighteenth-century sonatas to bear on the debate between Hepokoski and Darcy and Rosen, arguing that there is much to

---

2. Sisman, *Mozart*, 77.

3. Charles Rosen, *Sonata Forms*, rev. ed. (New York: W. W. Norton, 1988), 289; see also 106.

4. Rosen, *Sonata Forms*, 289.

5. James Hepokoski and Warren Darcy, *Elements of Sonata Theory: Norms, Types, and Deformations in the Late-Eighteenth-Century Sonata* (New York: Oxford University Press, 2006), 235.

6. Hepokoski and Darcy, *Elements of Sonata Theory*, 235–36.

learn about the emergence of sonata form from the history of the secondary development. Using examples by Carl Philipp Emanuel Bach and by Leopold and the young Wolfgang Amadeus Mozart, I will demonstrate that these flat-side leaning passages were as old as sonata form. I will argue that these examples require us to revise our understanding of the double return of the principal theme in the principal key in early cases of sonata form, as well as our expectations of what should occur after that return.

The Secondary Development as Part of the Recapitulation

But first, let us examine the assumptions that underlie some of the most influential approaches to the "Secondary Development section." Rosen, in coining the term, implies two things: first, that the kind of activity we witness at these points is characteristic of development sections; and second, that it is separated from the activity we witnessed before the double return and should therefore be considered "secondary." He implies what is an almost axiomatic assumption about sonata form, that the double return signifies the onset of a separate, third section of the form charged with "the affirmation of a large stable area," the recapitulation. Rosen interprets the Secondary Development section as using "techniques of harmonic and motivic development not to prolong the tension of the exposition, but to reinforce the resolution on the tonic." He emphasizes its subordination to the role of the recapitulation as a whole—a large-scale manifestation of the tonic.[7]

William Caplin's view, although different from Rosen's, likewise subjugates the secondary development to the role of the recapitulation as a whole. For Caplin, the secondary development is the consequence of the application of sequential repetition, or what he terms "model-sequence technique" to the double return. In Caplin's view, this is a response to the fact that most of the original roles of the first theme in the exposition, such as presenting the theme and establishing the home key by means of a cadence, "are no longer required or even necessarily appropriate," because by this point the main theme has already been heard and the home key reestablished at the end of the development.[8] Hence it is reasonable to assume that the double return should be the model rather than the sequence, and that a section of instability following a brief double return should only be possible after an adequate reestablishment of the home key.

Hepokoski and Darcy's attribution of the raison d'être of secondary development to a "quick fix" of the exposition once again situates it as a recapitulatory technique, both in function and in origin. Curiously, their critique of Rosen appears in and is limited

---

7. Rosen, *Sonata Forms*, 106.

8. William E. Caplin, *Classical Form: A Theory of Formal Functions for the Instrumental Music of Haydn, Mozart, and Beethoven* (New York: Oxford University Press, 1998), 161.

to their description of the recapitulatory transition, whereas Rosen's observation that "the Secondary Development as often as not returns to one of the themes of the *first* group" allows for its occurrence within the recapitulatory primary-theme zone.[9] Although Hepokoski and Darcy recognize the "synecdochic strategy" of beginning the "recapitulatory zone with enough of an incipit to recall the corresponding zone of the exposition," followed by a significant reworking of that zone, they claim (incorrectly, as we will see) that this practice is exceptional to Joseph Haydn.[10] By identifying the secondary development with the recapitulatory transition zone, and by explaining its existence as deriving from the functional "tweaks" that had to be made to that zone, Hepokoski and Darcy, like Rosen and Caplin, explain the secondary development as the consequence of the role of the recapitulation.

Yet as a number of recent studies have argued, the onset of the double return did not always have the baggage associated with an entire recapitulation.[11] In many mid-century works, a double return was a means of highlighting a local touching upon the tonic rather than the ultimate return to it. Thematically, it did not necessarily imply the commencement of a rotation, and many double returns were followed by new material, as in the Allegro from Johann Sebastian Bach's Sonata in E Major for Flute and Continuo, BWV 1035. There, although the double return declares the commencement of a final tonic section, it is not followed by anything like the strict correspondence to the exposition that we would expect to see in a sonata-form recapitulation (see example 2.1).[12]

The double return in this example may not have signified the onset of a rotation, but it nevertheless announced a final section firmly rooted in the tonic. J. S. Bach's practice

9. Rosen, *Sonata Forms*, 289.

10. Hepokoski and Darcy, *Elements of Sonata Theory*, 233.

11. Peter A. Hoyt, "The 'False Recapitulation' and the Conventions of Sonata Form" (PhD diss., University of Pennsylvania, 1999), 330–46; Markus Neuwirth, "Verschleierte Reprisen bei Joseph Haydn," in *Joseph Haydn (1732–1809)*, ed. Sebastian Urmoneit (Berlin: Weidler, 2009), 33–66; Markus Neuwirth, "Reprisenphänomene in den frühen Streichquartetten Joseph Haydns und Franz Asplmayers: Anmerkungen zu einem anachronistischen Sonatenform-Paradigma," in *Kammermusik im Übergang vom Barock zur Klassik*, ed. Christoph-Hellmut Mahling (Mainz: Villa Musica Rheinland-Pfalz, 2009), 95–124; Yoel Greenberg, "Of Beginnings and Ends: A Corpus-Based Inquiry into the Rise of the Recapitulation," *Journal of Music Theory* 61, no. 2 (2017): 171–200; Yoel Greenberg, "Haydn's Early Altered Recapitulations as Evidence of Early Sonata-Form Logic," *Music Theory and Analysis* 5, no. 2 (2018): 168–89.

12. The use of stock sonata-form terminology in reference to any of the works in this essay must be taken with a grain of salt. By "exposition" I refer to the first half of a binary-form work; by "development," to the section between the beginning of the second half and the double return; and by "recapitulation" to the section from the double return onward.

Example 2.1. J. S. Bach, Sonata for Flute and Continuo, BWV 1035, mvt. 2 Allegro, comparison between exposition and recapitulation.

in this movement, although rare within his own works, which seldom make use of a double return, was nonetheless quite typical of that of many Italian composers in the 1730s and 1740s, in particular Giovanni Battista Sammartini. Yet in numerous other cases, mostly in works of German composers in the mid-eighteenth century, including some of the works of the young Mozart, the double return was employed differently. Perhaps the best example of this was in the works of C. P. E. Bach, whose sonatas are often seen as important precursors, if not early exemplars, of sonata form. As in BWV 1035, Emanuel Bach's double returns were frequently followed by an extensive span of new material, especially in his earlier works, although he invariably rounded them off with a substantial "end rhyme," matching the closing material of both halves.[13] Also unlike BWV 1035, in which the double return spanned eight measures, restating the entire opening phrase along with its repetition, Emanuel Bach's early double returns were usually exceedingly short, at times lasting no more than a measure or two. Furthermore, more often than not, they were unstable in their harmonic context, lacking the preparation that Caplin associates with the double return as a prerequisite for the secondary development, yet still followed by the kind of fragmentation, sequencing, and modulations that we normally associate with the development section.

C. P. E. Bach's Sonata in A Major, Wq 48/6 (1742)

The first movement of the sixth "Prussian Sonata," Wq 48/6, exemplifies this practice (see example 2.2). The movement opens with a two-measure idea in *piano*, followed by a *forte* flourish with grand chords, and a passage of triplets that appear to approach a I:PAC in measures 6–7.[14] Yet rather than complete the descent to a perfect cadence on A, the treble rises to a C-sharp and carries on spinning out triplets in an ever-rising sequence, ignoring the bass's repeated efforts to reinstate the cadence. The triplets eventually run out of steam (or keyboard space) in measure 12 and the music slows to a halt on a I:HC in measure 15. In terms of Heinrich Christoph Koch's *Hauptperiode* model, this opening elides the first and second *Absätze*, with the moment of

---

13. The term *end rhyme* was first coined by Douglass M. Green, in *Form in Tonal Music: An Introduction to Analysis* (New York: Holt, Rinehart, and Winston, 1965) and taken up by Leonard G. Ratner, in *Classic Music: Expression, Form, and Style* (New York: Schirmer, 1980). It roughly corresponds to Hepokoski and Darcy's postcrux area. See Hepokoski and Darcy, *Elements of Sonata Theory*, 239–41.

14. In this essay I will denote cadences using the following convention: I:PAC is a perfect authentic cadence in the tonic, that is, a cadence ending in a V-I motion in the bass, with the treble on 1 in the tonic. IAC is an imperfect authentic cadence, in which the treble does not come to rest on 1 (most often on 3). HC is a half cadence. Due to the possibility of modulations, the local tonic will be marked prior to the type of cadence. Hence, a ii:HC denotes a half cadence in the supertonic. For more complete definitions, consult Caplin, *Classical Form*, 253–56.

Example 2.2. C. P. E. Bach, Sonata in A Major, Wq 48/6, mvt. 1 Allegro, mm. 77–108.

elision providing the fuel for most of the second *Absatz*.[15] Surprisingly, the subsequent *Quintabsatz* in the dominant (mm. 16–27) begins with eight measures in the supertonic (mm. 16–23), before swerving toward the required V:HC in measure 27, after which comes a long *Schlußsatz*.

The second half begins with a restatement of the main theme in the dominant, yet quickly realizes the promise given in the first half, focusing extensively on the supertonic (mm. 59–81), and concluding with a bold ii:PAC, echoing the cadence from the end of the exposition (cf. mm. 79–80 to mm. 43–44).[16] At this point the main theme reappears in the supertonic, which immediately reinterprets itself as the dominant of the dominant, E (mm. 83–85), yet rather than lead on to E Major, which would have convincingly completed the expected retransition to the tonic, Emanuel Bach turns to the dominant minor, leading to a v:PAC in measure 89. It is at this point that the double return reappears, yet it lasts barely two measures before, in an exact transposition of measures 81–89, it reinterprets itself as a dominant of the subdominant, resulting in an IV:IAC in measures 96 and 98. This time the passagework continues through a chain of descending fifths, proceeding successfully to the dominant (mm. 105–7) in an exact repetition of the close of the home-key *Quintabsatz* from the exposition (cf. mm. 12–15 to mm. 104–8).

The overall ii-V-I-IV motion in two sequential units, the second "one step lower" than the first, is typical of Joseph Riepel's *Fonte* schema.[17] With the first event in each half of the *Fonte* a weak one, the double return, which appears at the start of the second half of the *Fonte*, is the weakest and least structural of the events in measures 81–98.[18]

15. Heinrich Christoph Koch, *Versuch einer Anleitung zur Composition* (Leipzig: Adam Friedrich Bohme, 1793), §101 and §128–47. Alternatively, measure 15 could be understood in terms of what Robert Winter has called a "bifocal close," or a proposed I:HC medial caesura (subsequently declined) in the terminology of Hepokoski and Darcy. See Robert S. Winter, "The Bifocal Close and the Evolution of the Viennese Classical Style," *JAMS* 42 (1989): 275–337; Hepokoski and Darcy, *Elements of Sonata Theory*, 23–40, 45. If the use of stock sonata-form terminology for the works examined here is problematic, then all the more so the use of sonata-theory concepts, which were formulated on the basis of norms and defaults decades later.

16. Although not the most common goal of C. P. E. Bach's development sections, the most common being the submediant, the mediant, and a half cadence in the tonic, the supertonic is not unheard of either (e.g., the first movement of the Sonata in E-flat Major, Wq 65/28). Unlike the more common options, which allow direct continuation to the tonic, voice-leading considerations necessitate a retransition to bring the ii:PAC back to the tonic.

17. Robert O. Gjerdingen, *Music in the Galant Style* (New York: Oxford University Press, 2007), 61–71, esp. 63.

18. Gjerdingen, *Music in the Galant Style*, 29.

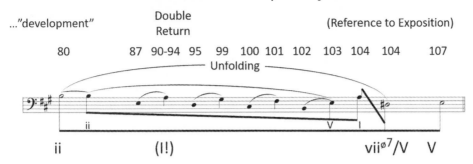

Figure 2.1. Voice-leading graph of bass in C. P. E. Bach,
Sonata in A Major, Wq 48/6, mvt. 1, mm. 80–107.

Table 2.1. Cycle of Fifths in C. P. E. Bach, Wq 48/6, mvt. 1, mm. 81–104

Measures	81–89	90–98	99–100	101–2	103–4	104	107
Harmony	ii (=V/v) v	I (=V/IV) IV	V/iii–iii	vi–ii	V–I	viiø7/V	V
Cycle of fifths in bass	B–E	A–D	G-sharp–C-sharp	F-sharp–B	E–A	D-sharp	E

Unlike the double return, the end rhyme in measures 112 and following is well prepared by a three-measure standing on the dominant in measures 105–7 (a repetition
of mm. 13–15), and hence it is only from the end rhyme that we sense an unequivocal
drive toward a cadence in the tonic, fully prepared and powerfully articulated.

A voice-leading graph (see figure 2.1) of the area before and after the double return
reinforces this impression: taken together, measures 81–107 consist of a cycle of fifths
leading from the supertonic to the dominant in ever shorter units (see table 2.1). As
figure 2.1 illustrates, the moment of the double return is not a structural tonic, but
rather a passing harmony within a larger fifth motion from the supertonic in measure
81 to the dominant in measure 103, a motion that is in itself subordinate to a larger
progression from the supertonic of the development section to the structural dominant
of measure 107. Although the tonic is momentarily highlighted by the appearance of
the main theme, its overall role suggests that it is nonstructural.[19] Instead, it is but a
small part of a larger retransition, from the point of furthest remove to the true return
to the tonic, which occurs around measure 112, where the end rhyme begins.

In light of the return to expositional material in the original key in measures 104–7,
the detour taken in measures 93–103 is gratuitous from a formal point of view. If the
double return would indeed signify the beginning of a recapitulation, the detour would

19. In fact, as table 2.1 implies, it is even less structural than the nonstructural tonic in m. 104.

make little or no sense. It could not have been understood as part of a large-scale tonic section—as Rosen, Caplin, and Hepokoski and Darcy propose to understand later post-double-return detours—because it fails to establish the tonic in any convincing way. It also fails to fulfill any of the criteria that Caplin proposed as enabling such detours: the tonic is unprepared at the end of the development, and although Bach uses the model-sequence technique here, the double return is not a model but rather the sequence. None of this is the result of a fault by the composer, but rather of the application of anachronistic sonata-form logic to a work composed in the early 1740s. If we were to free ourselves of the axiomatic association of the double return with the idea of a recapitulation, and instead understand this work in terms of binary form, the problem vanishes. Within binary forms, the tonic was expected to be touched upon in passing during the second half.[20] The ultimate return to the tonic would only occur toward the end; the tonic would be approached and established in the course of the end rhyme, similar to the way the dominant was approached in the first half. It would therefore be better to understand this work as a binary form with a double return highlighting a local passing through the tonic key, rather than as a sonata form with a recapitulation including a "secondary development."

Leopold Mozart's Sonata in B-flat Major, LMW XIII:2 (1762)

The sixth "Prussian Sonata," Wq 48/6, is not unique in C. P. E. Bach's output at that time. In both the "Prussian" (1742) and the "Württemberg" sets (1744), the double return was rarely prepared by any dominant, let alone a well-articulated one. It most often appeared after a hiatus following a cadence in the submediant or the mediant; it was more often than not less than four measures long (in one case, the first "Württemberg Sonata," Wq 49/1, lasting only a half a measure); and it was frequently incorporated as part of sequential activity, mostly afterward but sometimes, as in our case, before. Such weak double returns were characteristic of Bach's practice throughout the 1740s and 1750s: in more than two out of every three works, the double return is no longer than four measures.

Nor are weak double returns unique to C. P. E. Bach: they continued to be in vogue in the works of a variety of composers at least until the late 1760s.[21] The third movement of Leopold Mozart's Sonata in B-flat Major, composed in 1764, is a case in point. As opposed to Wq 48/6, in which the enormous development section was uncharacteristic of sonata-form proportions, Leopold Mozart's movement is more

---

20. A plethora of contemporary sources stating as much are quoted in Bella Brover-Lubovsky, "Le Diable Boiteux, Omnipresent Meyer, and 'Intermediate Tonic' in the Eighteenth-Century Symphony," *Indiana Theory Review* 26 (2005): 1–36. See also Hoyt, "False Recapitulation," 43, 65.

21. For examples by Haydn in the 1760s, see Greenberg, "Haydn's Early Altered Recapitulations."

sonata-like: the exposition, development, and recapitulation take up 36, 22, and 41 percent of the work, respectively. Yet here, too, a closer look at the double return suggests that an uncritical application of a sonata-form vocabulary may be unsuitable to such works.

The movement begins with a fourteen-measure phrase, structured as 4+4+4+2, which, as in the previous example, leads to a "bifocal close," or what Hepokoski and Darcy call an I:HC medial caesura (MC) in measure 14 (see example 2.3).[22] In this sonata the I:HC MC is not declined, but instead followed by a second theme based closely on the first. The essential expositional closure (EEC) is attained in measure 32, after which follow another eleven measures of cadential confirmation.[23] As is typical of many mid-century works, the second half begins by transposing the first twelve measures to the dominant, after which the development launches, roughly following the thematic sequence of events in most of the exposition but modulating to the submediant. The vi:PAC in measures 66–68 is thus a transposition to the submediant of the EEC in measures 30–32. Again, as is typical of works of that period, Mozart moves straight on to the double return (m. 69), through hiatus, with no retransition whatsoever. Yet the double return is both brief and unstable. It lasts little more than one measure, and is immediately destabilized, first by the bass in its second bar, which forgoes the dominant harmony from measure 2 in favor of the less stable first-inversion seventh, and then through the introduction of the flat seventh, bringing upon the customary tilt to the subdominant (example 2.4). And if in the previous example the double return was the continuation of a sequence, here the double return sets off a sequence structured along the lines of a two-part *Monte*, leading, as the *Monte* most commonly does, from subdominant to dominant (not the structural dominant, but a passing one; see figure 2.2).[24]

Even if Mozart's double return is the model for the sequence that follows it, it is nonetheless a far cry from a convincing establishment of the tonic. As figure 2.2 shows, in the overarching voice-leading scheme the *Monte* is part of a passing motion within

22. In Koch's terms, mm. 1–14 could be interpreted either as a four-measure *Grundabsatz* followed by a home-key *Quintabsatz*, or, as in Wq 48/6, as a work beginning with a *Quintabsatz*. The rest of the exposition would be understood as forgoing the *Quintabsatz* in the secondary key, and adding an appendix after the *Schlußabsatz*. In light of this rather clumsy description, I found sonata-theory terminology more appropriate to this example. The I:HC medial caesura introduces the secondary key area (or "S-space") by means of a caesura built around the dominant of the original tonic.

23. The EEC is usually the first satisfactory PAC within the secondary key that goes on to differing material or that closes the exposition itself; see Hepokoski and Darcy, *Elements of Sonata Theory*, 18 and n6.

24. Gjerdingen, *Music in the Galant Style*, 89–106.

Example 2.3. Leopold Mozart, Sonata in B-flat Major,
LMV XIII:2, mvt. 3 Allegro, mm. 1–18.

Example 2.4. Leopold Mozart Sonata in B-flat Major,
LMV XIII:2, mvt. 3 Allegro, mm. 67–92.

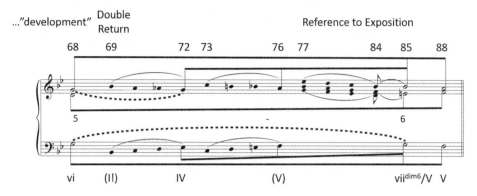

Figure 2.2. Voice-leading graph of Leopold Mozart, Sonata in B-flat Major, LMV XIII:2, mvt. 3, mm. 68–88.

a grand-scale double neighbor around the structural dominant in measure 88 (note how the entire progression is summarized in measures 85–86!).

As in example 2.4, the subdominant tilt following the double return cannot be understood as an adaptation of the exposition's materials to the different tonal trajectory of the recapitulation, because measures 77–80 (and then 81–84 an octave lower) replicate measures 5–8 in the original key. Instead, in the absence of a dominant preparation of the double return, both the double return and the subsequent subdominant become part of a drive to the powerful dominant that precedes the true final return to the tonic, the end rhyme. That dominant is the preparation for the final return to the tonic, which occurs with the end rhyme, in this case the commencement in measure 89 of the monothematic second theme from measure 15.

To bring us full circle, it is worth noting that two years after the composition of Leopold's sonata, the eight-year-old W. A. Mozart employs a similar strategy in the recapitulation of his Violin Sonata in F Major, K 13 (example 2.5). Like his father, Mozart arrives at the double return directly from a vi:PAC, only adding a brief connecting passage that might have been improvised by the keyboard player in Leopold's sonata anyway. From here on, the apple doesn't fall far from the tree, with the young Wolfgang's *Monte* less regular than his father's, but nonetheless quite identical in its implementation.

Conclusion: Between Extended Retransition and the Secondary Development

In the examples by Emanuel Bach and by the Mozarts, father and son, the double return does not signify the start of a closing section in the tonic, as we are accustomed to thinking of it in sonata form. Tonally, it is part of a retransition, leading from the

Example 2.5. W. A. Mozart, Violin Sonata in F Major, K 13, mvt. 1 Allegro, mm. 63–70.

point of furthest remove—the supertonic in the sonata by C. P. E. Bach and the sub-mediant in those by the Mozarts—to the structural dominant that prepares the true return to the tonic in the end rhyme. Rosen was correct in observing that the tilt to the subdominant does not serve as a "quick fix" to the exposition, but his interpretation of the role of that tilt in serving the consolidation of the tonic cannot apply to these works, where the tonic had not been established well enough to be consolidated. On the contrary, the tilt in these works serves to destabilize the tonic as part of its motion toward that structural dominant. The result is the opening up of a space shortly after the double return, during which we experience the type of instability that we do not usually associate with the recapitulation, but more normally with the development or the retransition.

Yet it would be a mistake to refer to this as a "secondary development" for two reasons. First, if the double return does not signify the start of a new, tonic-centered section, then the activity following it cannot be considered "secondary." Second, and somewhat paradoxically, the tonal trajectory of this section, leading from the point of furthest remove and gradually approaching the structural dominant, is not typical of the main part of the development, but rather of the retransition.

The examples examined here are typical in their handling of the double return of numerous works by a variety of composers until well into the 1770s. But this is not to say that similar incidences in later works, and in particular those by Wolfgang Mozart, should not be considered secondary developments. By Mozart's time, the double return had assumed a meaning, both harmonic and thematic, that it would not have had in the mid-eighteenth century.[25] It had become a structural moment that was most often strongly prepared by a forceful drive to and an insistent standing on the dominant, and even when it was not—such as the moment in which the sun emerges gently from behind a cloud, two measures before the recapitulation in the finale of the "Jupiter"

25. Greenberg, "Of Beginnings and Ends."

Symphony—it was an arresting enough moment to highlight the recapitulation as the beginning of something new.

Yet with the newly interpreted double return came the challenge of reinterpreting what had so often come after it. Within what was, by then, a clearly defined recapitulation, the recomposed sections with their flat-side tilts, frequently to the subdominant, and their quicksilver tonal shifts, could no longer serve the purpose they had served before, that of retransition, not least because the retransition had already taken place, and the tonic was well established. These sections now took on new meaning, allowing composers to readdress issues that remained open or unexplored in the development section, or to charge the potentially mechanical role of the recapitulation with music of striking originality. In Mozart, Beethoven, and many of Haydn's works, it is justifiable to refer to these recomposed sections as "secondary developments," yet we should be cautious when applying these terms to earlier works, such as those by mid-century composers, or even early Haydn or Mozart. And perhaps this shifting history of a complex practice should serve as a caution against applying context-dependent terms such as "secondary" and "development" to moments that could have been perceived as neither.

A Pursuit of Wealth

The Freelance Endeavors of
Bach and Mozart

Noelle M. Heber

Apursuit of wealth may not be the primary impetus for most musicians when they choose a career in music, and it certainly would not have been the key motivating factor for Johann Sebastian Bach or Wolfgang Amadeus Mozart. It was clear from an early point in both of their lives that being born into a musical family *and* possessing an obvious musical talent set them on their respective vocational journeys. Accordingly, while family and talent undoubtedly prompted their individual paths to pursuing music as a vocation, they both clearly had to navigate the practical reality of earning a living. Some modern-day enthusiasts may not be open to the idea that a musical genius may have composed more for practical purposes than from pure inspiration.[1] Nevertheless, the need for money was indeed a reality that should inform our understanding of these historical figures.

Bach and Mozart emerged from distinctive economic circumstances, but a survey of their independent endeavors as musicians reveals some striking similarities. Both composers at some point in their careers benefitted from a fixed income at a royal court. Both likewise bemoaned a lack of money in personal correspondence while living in expensive cities and carrying the responsibility of supporting their families. Bach was an innovative freelancer, pursuing independent work in addition to his salaried positions. His activities included guest performances, organ examinations, direction of the Collegium Musicum in Leipzig, publication of his own compositions, and operation of a book and instrument sales and rental service. Mozart relied on freelance work as his main source of income while living in Vienna, where he for the most part did not have a fixed salary. Among his freelance activities were concert performances,

---

1. See Neal Zaslaw, "Mozart as a Working Stiff," in *On Mozart*, ed. James M. Morris (Cambridge: Cambridge University Press, 1994), 102–12. See also Daniel K. L. Chua, "Myth: Mozart, Money, Music," in *Mozart Studies*, ed. Simon P. Keefe (Cambridge: Cambridge University Press, 2006), 193–213.

operas, and commissions. Teaching private music lessons to wealthy amateurs provided a lucrative side job for both musicians. Available documents and previous scholarly evaluations of each individual's financial situation allow for a fascinating comparison of the fluctuating earnings of two eighteenth-century composers who achieved a measure of financial success through their independent pursuits. Whether motivated by more artistic freedom, independence, reputation, necessity, or greater earning potential, Bach and Mozart boldly sought opportunities for freelance work.

In written correspondence one finds mention of a "pursuit of wealth" among both composers' individual aims. In Bach's famous letter to Georg Erdmann in 1730, in which he complained about an insufficient and unstable salary and conflict with authorities in Leipzig, he voiced a desire to "seek his fortune elsewhere":

> Here, by God's will, I am still in service. But since (1) I find that the post is by no means so lucrative as it was described to me; (2) I have failed to obtain many of the fees pertaining to the office; (3) the place is very expensive; and (4) the authorities are odd and little interested in music, so that I must live amid almost continual vexation, envy, and persecution; accordingly I shall be forced, with God's help, to seek my fortune elsewhere.[2]

Mozart used similar language in a letter written on 1 August 1777, in which he asked the Archbishop Colloredo in Salzburg, his current employer at the time, for permission to travel in order to make money:

> Your grace will not misunderstand this petition, seeing that when I asked you for permission to travel to Vienna three years ago, you graciously declared that I had nothing to hope for in Salzburg and would do better to seek my fortune elsewhere.[3]

The words here translated "fortune" in English would have carried a general implication of "luck" in the original language; Bach used the Latin-derived "Fortun" while Mozart employed the German word "Glück." While both letters indicate that money was a *part* of the sought-after "fortune," the word itself encompasses more than wealth, as it can refer to one's overall well-being as contrasted with "misfortune" and carries a sense of circumstances being directed by God.[4] This essay nevertheless explores the pursuit of wealth itself as a specific, tangible intention that "fortune" clearly encompasses here. Although the title of this essay may be somewhat provocative, it

2. NBR, 151–52, no. 152; BDOK 1:67–68, no. 23. For an elaboration on the working conditions in Leipzig that would have motivated this letter, see Michael Maul, *Bach's Famous Choir: The Saint Thomas School in Leipzig, 1212–1804*, trans. Richard Howe (Woodbridge, UK: Boydell Press, 2018), 141–207.

3. LMF, 268; MBA, 2:5. The petition was written by Leopold but signed by Wolfgang.

4. Johann Heinrich Zedler, *Grosses vollständiges Universal-Lexicon aller Wissenschafften und Künste*, s.v. "Glück" (Halle, 1731–54), vol. 10, col. 1701.

highlights the freelance possibilities and endeavors that the two composers pursued in order to earn income in addition to other employment opportunities.

Bach and Mozart both expressed frustration over financial matters elsewhere in their personal correspondence.[5] These accounts do not necessarily provide an objective or unique perspective,[6] but they have nevertheless played a role in popular notions about Bach and Mozart as financially lacking or even "poor," ideas that have shifted over time. In 1908, Albert Schweitzer wrote that Bach's income could not have been a modest one, while the same year, Carl Seffner's gallant sculpture of Bach with an outturned pocket was inaugurated next to the Thomaskirche in Leipzig; some locals today inform visitors that his pocket was turned out to indicate that Bach was always lacking money. Ideas about Mozart living in poverty were challenged some time ago. An article in 1991 sought to dispel a common misconception portrayed in Peter Shaffer's popular movie *Amadeus* that Mozart was left unrewarded for his genius and died a pauper.[7] Although complaints from Bach or Mozart about insufficient pay would have been subjective, they do reflect a society in which employment norms were shifting for musicians and composers. Finding more earning potential was not an easy path, whether one always remained regularly employed as Bach did or, like Mozart, decided to risk everything to become an independent musician.

The financial situations of Bach and Mozart have been reevaluated over the years and yet incomplete documentation continues to limit the conclusions that can be drawn.[8] This essay builds on previous scholarly work focused on each composer's individual financial situation and brings a new perspective to the evolution of independent work

---

5. For example, in addition to his letter to Erdmann, see Bach's letters to the king concerning insufficient pay for services at the university church (NBR, 118–25, nos. 119–20; BDOK 1:30–41, nos. 9–12; BDOK 2:149, 155, nos. 192, 202) and further examples discussed in Noelle M. Heber, *J. S. Bach's Material and Spiritual Treasures: A Theological Perspective* (Woodbridge, UK: Boydell Press, 2021), 229–40.

6. According to Andrew Talle, "German archives are full of letters from both court and city musicians begging their employers for more money." *Beyond Bach: Music and Everyday Life in the Eighteenth Century* (Urbana: University of Illinois Press, 2017), 218.

7. Peter Passel, "Economic Scene: Mozart's Money Misunderstanding," *New York Times*, 11 December 1991, https://www.nytimes.com/1991/12/11/business/economic-scene-mozart-s-money-misunderstanding.html. For another analysis of the movie, including its positive influence, see Robert L. Marshall, "Mozart and *Amadeus*," in *Bach and Mozart: Essays on the Enigma of Genius* (Rochester, NY: University of Rochester Press, 2019), 197–211 (originally published in *Musical Quarterly* 81 (1997): 173–79).

8. Recent analyses of Bach's and Mozart's respective financial situations can be found in Heber, *Bach's Material and Spiritual Treasures*, 15–61; and Jessica Waldoff, "Mozart and Finances," in *Mozart in Context*, ed. Simon P. Keefe (Cambridge: Cambridge University Press, 2019), 170–80. See also Maynard Solomon, *Mozart: A Life* (New York: HarperCollins, 1995), 521–28.

among musicians in the eighteenth century. By comparing these two figures side by side, it highlights the freelancing challenges and opportunities of each composer in their distinct historical and geographical settings, and also questions some of the stereotypes about these two individuals in particular.

The comparison of these two composers is particularly useful for the topic of emerging freelancing endeavors among musicians. Perhaps the most obvious distinction is that Bach and Mozart represent the two great "genius" composers of the eighteenth century. This coupling is not original: Robert L. Marshall rationalizes his pairing choice in part by what each composer represents in the greater context of music history: "According to the traditional view, Bach's music was the culmination of the so-called Baroque era during the first half of the century; Mozart's, conversely, was the culmination of the antithetical Classical style, during the second half."[9] Bach and Mozart represent two distinctive prototypes among the many pioneering freelance musicians of their time, and Mozart's efforts in particular would pave the way for future generations of musicians. Juxtaposing their freelance activities underscores both enduring similarities and developments among musicians over the course of two generations. This essay thus highlights how Bach and Mozart encountered both success and disappointment in their pursuit of freelance activities at distinct phases of an evolving economy for musicians, focusing primarily on the years during which they were most active as freelancers: Bach's tenure as cantor in Leipzig (1723–50) and Mozart's Vienna years (1781–91).

Two Distinct Settings

Bach and Mozart emerged from dissimilar backgrounds and family situations. Bach's parents died by the time he was ten years old, and he thereafter relied on the goodwill of family members and scholarships for his upbringing and education; he was financially independent by the age of fifteen. Bach never left Germany nor actively pursued an international career, although the international fairs in Leipzig brought people from other European countries to his doorstep. Mozart, in contrast, was brought up in a more privileged household. His father was *very* present in his life, even well into his adulthood, and took him abroad on concert tours as a child prodigy. The young Mozart had become known outside of Austria before reaching maturity and sought employment opportunities in foreign countries as an adult.

---

9. Marshall, *Bach and Mozart*, 186; chapter 12, "Bach and Mozart: Styles of Musical Genius" (originally published in *BACH: Journal of the Riemenschneider Bach Institute* 22 [1991]: 16–32) includes comparisons between Bach and Mozart from various aspects such as their personal lives, personalities, and musical styles.

The affluent cities of Leipzig and Vienna were both epicenters of intellectual thought and international convergence. Bach's tenure in Leipzig coincided with prominent Lutheran theologians who taught at the university while leaders of the German Pietist movement concurrently led church reforms in Leipzig and Halle. As the capital of the Habsburg Empire, Vienna accommodated numerous members of the nobility, and local intellectuals embraced the Enlightenment under the reign and reforms of Emperor Joseph II. The increasing prosperity of these cities meant that the cost of living presented a rising challenge, especially for musicians with fluctuating salaries or who relied on freelance activities. Bach and Mozart of course also carried the responsibility of providing for their wives and children.

Ascertaining the relationship between monetary units in Bach's Germany and Mozart's Austria is challenging due to their fluid values over the course of time and by location. In Germany, the primary monetary units and coins in use were thaler, gulden, groschen, and pfennig; in Austria and Bavaria, they were florins, kreuzer, and pfennig. As a general and imperfect conversion rate, the Austrian florin was worth roughly two-thirds of a German thaler.[10] (See table 3.1 for basic conversion rates.) A consideration of average salaries in the two contexts may be more helpful in appreciating the value of payments rendered to Bach and Mozart.

During Bach's time, average yearly salaries in Germany ranged from less than 40 thaler for village schoolteachers, 150–300 thaler for parish clergy, 200–400 thaler for university professors, and up to 600 thaler for bishops.[11] Court musicians in Dresden earned some impressive figures: Vice-Kapellmeister Johann David Heinicken earned 1,200 thaler, while Kapellmeister Antonio Lotti and his wife, the singer Santa Stella, were paid 10,500 thaler per year.[12] Bach himself started with fairly modest earnings, but

10. See W. H. Bruford, *Germany in the Eighteenth Century: The Social Background of the Literary Revival* (Cambridge: Cambridge University Press, 1959), 329–30.

11. Bruford, *Germany in the Eighteenth Century*, 249–50; M. J. Elsas, *Umriss einer Geschichte der Preise und Löhne in Deutschland: Vom ausgehenden Mittelalter bis zum Beginn des neunzehnten Jahrhunderts*, vol. 2, pt. A (Leiden: Sijthoff, 1940), 625–26.

12. Richard Petzoldt, "The Economic Conditions of the 18th-Century Musician," in *The Social Status of the Professional Musician from the Middle Ages to the 19th Century*, ed. Walter Salmen, trans. Herbert Kaufman and Barbara Reisner (New York: Pendragon Press, 1983), 159–88, esp. 166. See also Christoph Wolff, *Johann Sebastian Bach: The Learned Musician* (New York: W. W. Norton, 2000), 183; *Bachs Welt: Sein Leben, Sein Schaffen, Seine Zeit: Festschrift für Henning Müller-Buscher zum 70. Geburtstag*, ed. Siegbert Rampe (Laaber: Laaber Verlag, 2015), 146. See also Janice B. Stockigt, "The Court of Saxony-Dresden," in *Music at German Courts, 1715–1760: Changing Artistic Priorities*, ed. Samantha Owens, Barbara M. Reul, and Janice B. Stockigt (Woodbridge, UK: Boydell Press, 2011), 17–49, esp. 24 and table 2.1.

Table 3.1. Currency Conversion in Germany
and Austria in the Eighteenth Century

Germany	
One groschen	= 12 pfennig
One florin/gulden	= 21 groschen
One thaler	= 24 groschen
Austria	
One kreuzer	= 4 pfennig
One florin/gulden	= 60 kreuzer

his salary improved with every change of position. In Weimar, where he was employed as a court organist, chamber musician, and eventually Konzertmeister from 1708 to 1717, Bach received an increasing yearly salary, starting at 150 florins and mounting to 250 florins, including growing allowances of wood and coal.[13] His initial salary as court Kapellmeister in Cöthen was 400 thaler.[14]

Bach indeed complained about his salary in Leipzig in 1730, which he estimated to total about 700 thaler, even though he presumably would have been assured of 1,000–1,200 thaler yearly when he accepted the position.[15] His frustration in 1730 was influenced by numerous factors, of which a fluctuating salary was one. Only his base payment of 100 thaler a year was stable; the fees from legacies, services for funerals and weddings, and maintenance of church instruments varied considerably from year to year.[16] Yet the fact that he remained in Leipzig until his death twenty years later is probably at least partially due to the city's potential for independent work; its book publishers would print some of his music, local international fairs would help him to distribute it, and the university would bring him wealthy amateur music students.[17] The smaller cities of Weimar and Cöthen, where he was previously employed as a court musician, would not have afforded the same opportunities.

13. NBR, 59–61, 70, 73, nos. 35–36, 38–39, 51, 57; BDOK 2:35–37, 53, 57, nos. 38–41, 66, 73.

14. From 1721, Anna Magdalena also earned a yearly salary of 200 thaler; see BDOK 2:67–68, no. 86. An increased salary of 300 thaler per year has often been misreported, for example, in NBR, 93–94, no. 87; see Andrew Talle, "Who Was Anna Magdalena Bach?" *BACH: Journal of the Riemenschneider Bach Institute* 41, no. 1 (2020): 139–71, esp. 141.

15. Wolff, *The Learned Musician*, 492n24; Hans-Joachim Schulze, *Bach-Facetten: Essays, Studien, Miszellen* (Stuttgart: Evangelische Verlagsanstalt, 2017), 46–47.

16. Bach's base salary consisted of eighty-seven thaler, twelve groschen plus thirteen thaler, three groschen in the form of "Wood and Light Money," paid quarterly. He also received free housing. NBR, 110, no. 108; BDOK 2:102, 119–20, 335–36, nos. 137, 157, 435.

17. See Heber, *Bach's Material and Spiritual Treasures*, 37–57.

Average salaries in Mozart's context demonstrate a similar scope: 10–60 florins for domestic servants, 120–300 florins for schoolteachers, less than 400 florins for professional orchestral musicians, 200–1,000 florins for middle-class professionals, and 600–3,000 florins for university professors.[18] Members of the nobility and government officials would have earned significantly more. Mozart's financial journey was more precarious than Bach's—only twice did he benefit from a fixed salary in a court; otherwise he earned money according to his professional engagements. His European music tours as a child in the 1760s and 1770s brought him fame as a performer, but not much financial benefit. In between his absences from his hometown of Salzburg in the 1770s, he was employed as a court musician where he earned a yearly salary of 150 florins. Toward the end of that decade, Mozart set out on a trip to look for employment in Munich, Mannheim, and Paris from September 1777 to January 1779. When this quest proved to be unsuccessful, he returned to Salzburg where his court appointment as Organist-Konzertmeister offered a more favorable salary of 450 florins.

Mozart was not satisfied with this salaried position, but his search for a more acceptable court appointment had been unsuccessful, especially since Kapellmeister positions were rapidly declining at the time.[19] As a result, freelancing seemed to be the most obvious path toward more artistic freedom and greater earning potential. Mozart was optimistic about the prospects of freelancing in Vienna. On 8 April 1781, shortly after arriving in the capital, he tried to persuade his father that it was in his best interest to leave the archbishop's service, writing, "I should give a grand concert, take four pupils, and in a year I should have got on so well in Vienna that I could make at least a thousand thalers a year."[20] Mozart subsequently launched his freelance career in Vienna and relied on a variety of activities for his income from 1781 to 1791. His second court position was finally secured during these years; from 1787, he was hired as Kammerkompositeur by Emperor Joseph II, for which he received a yearly salary of 800 florins for light obligations.[21]

18. P. G. M. Dickson, *Finance and Government under Maria Theresia: 1740–1780*, vol. 2, *Finance and Credit* (Oxford: Clarendon Press, 1987), 63–64.

19. Julia Moore, "Mozart in the Market-Place," *Journal of the Royal Musical Association* 114, no. 1 (1989): 18–42, esp. 40.

20. LMF, 722; MBA, 3:104.

21. MDB, 306; MDL, 269–70. For more on this position and Mozart's probable future potential in this court had he lived longer, see Christoph Wolff, *Mozart at the Gateway to His Fortune* (New York: W. W. Norton, 2012), 9–21.

The Rise of Freelancing Activity among
Composers in the Eighteenth Century

Scholars have marked both Bach and Mozart individually as freelancing forerunners. Christoph Wolff remarks, "Toward the end of his life Bach came astonishingly close to the romantic ideal of the freelance artist."[22] According to Norbert Elias, the music market for freelance composers was "only just beginning" during Mozart's time.[23] In reality, the freelance activities of Bach and Mozart did not set them apart as lone pioneers but rather represented a broader trend among musicians of their time. Their uniqueness is tied to the success they achieved during their lifetimes and the enduring quality of their compositions. An informative study by F. M. Scherer highlights the development of freelance activity among composers born between 1650 and 1849.[24] Scherer proposes that "a transition from patronage-oriented to market-oriented free-lance composition did occur, but that it was much more gradual and evolutionary than the focus on Mozart as a turning point implies. Antecedents can be found a century before the death of Mozart. And nearly a century after his death, remnants of the old system survived."[25]

Scherer traces declining support from the nobility, waning employment in churches, and the concurrent rise of freelance activity between 1650 and 1849. His data, showing that employment for composers within courts and churches dropped significantly in the second half of the eighteenth century, supports the experiences of our two famous prototypes from this era; Bach remained employed until his death, while Mozart failed to find satisfactory employment opportunities and as a result, spent most of his adult life working independently.[26] Scherer shows that Bach was not alone in initial freelance activity, since a significant number of contemporary composers born between 1650 and 1699 engaged in freelance work. Freelance composition then increased steadily throughout the eighteenth and nineteenth centuries. Among the political, social, and economic developments that paved the way for increased freelance activity, there was growing demand for music lessons, printed sheet music, and quality instruments among middle-class families who wanted their children to learn music.

22. Christoph Wolff, *Bach: Essays on his Life and Music* (Cambridge, MA: Harvard University Press, 1991), 40.

23. Norbert Elias, *Mozart: Portrait of a Genius*, trans. Edmund Jephcott (Berkeley: University of California Press, 1993), 29.

24. F. M. Scherer, *Quarter Notes and Bank Notes: The Economics of Music Composition in the Eighteenth and Nineteenth Centuries* (Princeton, NJ: Princeton University Press, 2004), 8–9.

25. Scherer, *Quarter Notes*, 2.

26. Scherer, *Quarter Notes*, 67–78. See also William J. Baumol and Hilda Baumol, "On the Economics of Musical Composition in Mozart's Vienna," *Journal of Cultural Economics* 18 (1994): 171–98.

Retrospective views of this shift from employment opportunities to financial inde-pendence for eighteenth-century composers are often painted idealistically, accenting increased freedom and improved social status for musicians who were previously lim-ited by employment in the municipal sphere and in courts. Yet despite the limitations, there were certain job perks to employment, which usually included a fixed annual salary, free housing, other daily provisions, and a pension during old age. In fact, some of the first "freelance" musicians—those who found a way to earn money from music entertainment outside of these structures—were at the time of Bach not practicing an ideal profession: "They were looked upon with contempt by the steadily employed musicians who called them *Bratengeiger* and *Bierfiedler* [roast or beer violinists] be-cause they often played at festive meals."[27] While composers such as Bach would have achieved a higher social status compared to this lower-end extreme, the categories were not clearly defined. According to Andrew Talle, "In one way or another, Bach and his professional colleagues faced fundamental questions about the value of their work every day. . . . Music's ambiguous status was a burden for its practitioners, from boys first approaching their parents about pursuing professional careers to elderly retirees."[28] Musicians from Bach's time often came from the artisan classes, had fam-ily members who were professional musicians, and were either apprenticed as musi-cians or attended a choir school, while some chose to pursue university education.[29] A closer look reveals great variety in how employed musicians ranked socially, how much freedom they enjoyed, and the other nonmonetary provisions that were tied to employment.

The status and recognition of church organists in Lutheran Germany during Bach's time varied from place to place, where jobs were at times obtained through marriage or cash donations (such as in Hamburg, where the organist paying the largest sum, as a sort of bribe, would win the job), and prospects in smaller cities were poor.[30] Can-tors carried out an assortment of responsibilities including teaching, composition, and performances, and their status in society was unclear. Tanya Kevorkian describes their social status as follows:

> Cantors did not fit neatly into the main urban groupings of the elites, burghers, and
> sub-burghers. Scholars have argued that cantors' cultural standing conveyed a higher

27. Petzoldt, "The Economic Conditions of the 18th-Century Musician," 166.

28. Talle, *Beyond Bach*, 208.

29. Talle, *Beyond Bach*, 208–11.

30. Arnfried Edler, "The Social Status of Organists in Lutheran Germany from the 16th through the 19th Century," in *The Social Status of the Professional Musician*, ed. Salmen, 61–93, esp. 86–87; NBR, 89–90, no. 81; BDOK 2:77–78, no. 102; Talle, *Beyond Bach*, 214.

social status than their income and some aspects of their job descriptions would indicate. . . . As they did elsewhere, they shared some features with clerics: unless they
owned homes of their own in the city, they were not burghers; they, like clerics, lived
in service apartments; and both occupations were exempt from military and watch
duty. However, a cantor's status was complicated by ties to the material conditions of
schools and his duties there.[31]

Nevertheless, the more high-profile positions, such as Bach's post in Leipzig, afforded
the cantors and organists who obtained them greater prestige, higher salaries, and
increased opportunities for earning extra income.[32] In contrast with Vienna, sacred
music continued to play an important role in Leipzig after Bach's time, where church
music influenced the rise of public concerts, and other prominent musicians would
occupy the ecclesiastical role of Thomaskantor.[33]

Bach and Mozart both experienced periods of employment as court musicians, who
generally had a low rank in the court system.[34] Mozart was not thrilled about sharing
meals with servants while visiting Vienna in the service of Archbishop Colloredo.[35]
Indeed, the ranks and salaries of court musicians varied considerably and often included
nonmonetary forms of compensation such as accommodation, perishable goods, and
other benefits and allowances.[36] Nevertheless, being employed by the nobility did not
always ensure job security, since court musicians could be dismissed at any time or
could lose their positions when patrons died or when a court altered its financial priorities.[37] Furthermore, musicians needed permission to leave their patron's service. This
restriction affected both Bach and Mozart: Bach was imprisoned for almost a month
at the end of 1717 by Duke Wilhelm Ernst when Bach insisted on being released from

31. Tanya Kevorkian, *Baroque Piety: Religion, Society, and Music in Leipzig, 1650–1750* (Aldershot, UK:
Ashgate, 2007), 126.

32. See Talle, *Beyond Bach*, 222–56, regarding Carl August Hartung, whose social status and earning
potential improved upon taking the position of organist in Braunschweig in 1760.

33. Jeffrey S. Sposato, *Leipzig after Bach: Church and Concert Life in a German City* (Oxford: Oxford
University Press, 2018), 11; for more on the development of the music culture and the role of sacred
and secular enterprises in Leipzig after Bach, see chapter 2, "Church Music and the Rise of the Public
Concert, 1743–1785," 82–154.

34. Talle, *Beyond Bach*, 212.

35. See Mozart's letters from 17 and 24–28 March and 4 April 1781 in lmf, 713–14, 716–21; mba,
3:93–95, 97–103.

36. See Petzoldt, "The Economic Conditions of the 18th-Century Musician"; and Steven Zohn, "'Die
vornehmste Hof-Tugend': German Musicians' Reflections on Eighteenth-Century Court Life," in
Music at German Courts, ed. Owens, Reul, and Stockigt, 413–25.

37. Zohn, "Die vornehmste Hof-Tugend," 417.

service in Weimar.[38] And Mozart, after violating his employment contract when he left the service of Colloredo, two years later feared being arrested if he were to return to Salzburg for a visit, especially since he had not yet received a formal dismissal.[39] As evidenced by Bach's move from a court position to the cantorate in Leipzig and similar tendencies among other contemporaries (such as Georg Philipp Telemann rejecting a lucrative court position in Dresden), there was an appeal to holding a municipal music position.[40] Talle summarizes these challenges as follows: "Relationships between musicians and patrons at court were sharply asymmetrical; court musicians were at the mercy of the wild mood swings of inbred potentates, subjected to abuse of all kinds, and not always paid. Musicians and other employees deemed unfaithful, recalcitrant, or simply too talkative could be interrogated, jailed, or worse."[41]

During the second half of the eighteenth century, significant changes in the relationships between patrons and composers developed as members of the nobility were increasingly hiring musicians for single concerts and compositions rather than engaging them for long-term exclusive employment. While Mozart found the archbishop of Salzburg—who followed the former patronage trend—to be too restrictive, he in turn benefited from the new style of arrangements, such as the concerts organized by his patrons Prince Dmitry Golitsin and Gottfried Baron van Swieten in Vienna.[42] Concert life in Vienna continued to rely on the support of the nobility—and the prestige accompanying that support—even as it became more public.[43] In contrast to the prominent view that the rise of the public concert resulted from an economic downfall of the aristocracy, which disbanded the Kapellen, the nobility in fact continued to play an essential role in the promotion and support of musicians even through the reorganization of musical life.[44] The new structure resulted in more independent musicians but at the same time initially put them in a more tenuous economic situation, since

38. *nbr*, 80, no. 68; *bdok* 2:65–66, no. 84.

39. Letter of 21 May 1783 in *lmf*, 849; *mba*, 3:270.

40. Zohn, "Die vornehmste Hof-Tugend," 418–19.

41. Talle, *Beyond Bach*, 213.

42. John A. Rice, *Music in the Eighteenth Century* (New York: W. W. Norton, 2013), 205–6. For more on the relationship dynamics between musicians and patrons as exemplified in composition dedications, see Emily H. Green, *Dedicating Music, 1785–1850* (Rochester, NY: University of Rochester Press, 2019), 41–76.

43. See Rice, *Music in the Eighteenth Century*, 205–11; and David Gramit, *Cultivating Music: The Aspirations, Interests, and Limits of German Musical Culture, 1770–1848* (Berkeley: University of California Press, 2002), 11–12, 145–47.

44. Tia DeNora, *Beethoven and the Construction of Genius: Musical Politics in Vienna, 1792–1803* (Berkeley: University of California Press, 1997), 37–59.

they lost employment benefits such as noncash forms of remuneration. Musicians in Vienna in the 1790s thus continued to rely on wealthy aristocrats for their reputations and financial survival:

> Whereas success in London was dependent more on the patronage of fellow musicians (and public concert organizers and impresarios), in Vienna it was virtually impossible for a local musician to build a successful concert career without the patronage of individual aristocratic concert hosts. . . . Without previous private backing from aristocratic patrons, a musician found that the already scarce opportunities to present himself 'to the public' became virtually nonexistent.[45]

Consequently, the situation for eighteenth-century musicians—even prominent ones—was precarious, and their social and economic status varied according to time, place, and position. Within this framework, my discussion now turns to the specific freelance endeavors of Bach and Mozart; while the nature of their activities was similar, including concerts, teaching, and publication of their compositions, the milieus varied.

Performances, Commissions, and Other Professional Engagements

According to Scherer, "The form of freelance activity with the strongest element of entrepreneurship is acting as impresario, supervising and organizing the performance of one's own or others' musical works and acting as residual risk-bearer, reaping the profits if the performance succeeds economically and incurring the losses if it does not."[46] J. S. Bach was less active as an impresario than some of his contemporaries, such as Antonio Vivaldi, Telemann, and George Frideric Handel.[47] In fact, most of Bach's musical activities entailed little if any personal financial risk. These included guest performances, organ examinations and consultations, commissions for special events, and direction of the Collegium Musicum performances. Some of Bach's better-paid gigs include 60 thaler for a guest performance at the Cöthen court (1724), 230 thaler for a performance at Cöthen for Prince Leopold's funeral (1729), 160 thaler for an organ examination at Kassel (1732), and 58 thaler for a cantata performance for the king's visit to Leipzig (1738). It should be noted, however, that most of these figures included travel expenses. Payment records are far from complete, but Bach's fees did increase over time.[48]

45. DeNora, *Beethoven*, 55.

46. Scherer, *Quarter Notes*, 74.

47. Scherer, *Quarter Notes*, 75.

48. For a full list of Bach's known organ examinations and guest performances and the corresponding payments, when available, see table 1.7 in Heber, *Bach's Material and Spiritual Treasures*, 40–44.

Mozart was a proper impresario in Vienna, where he organized some of his own public and private concerts, rented the concert halls himself, and found considerable success from the endeavor during his first years in Vienna.[49] One of his self-organized public concerts took place in the Burgtheater each year during Lent. There is little information available concerning the expenses and revenue for these concerts, but Leopold Mozart once reported a profit of 559 gulden for his son's concert at the Mehlgrube.[50]

Mozart furthermore organized lower-risk subscription concerts, for which he would announce the program in advance and sell tickets for a series of three or six concerts. If there were adequate subscriptions, he would then hire orchestra players and rent the hall; otherwise the series could be canceled.[51] This pursuit proved to be profitable in some instances: Mozart's revenue, including expenses, apparently totaled 1,044 florins for three subscription concerts at the Trattnerhof in 1784 and 2,025 florins for six subscriptions concerts at the Mehlgrube in 1785.[52] However, after Mozart had announced another series in 1789 and secured only one subscriber, he canceled the concerts and dodged a financial loss.[53]

Mozart also performed frequently for the nobility in private settings, although payments fluctuated: he received 225 florins from the emperor for a competition with Clementi in 1781, 450 florins from the elector of Saxony for a concert in 1789, and 135 florins for a concert from the elector of Mainz in 1790.[54] On other occasions, payment came in the form of gifts, which Mozart did not particularly appreciate.[55] Unfortunately, Mozart's popularity as a pianist waned in the mid-1780s, in part because "the time span during which a particular artist was in demand was relatively short, since the semi-social private world thrived on the newest and the most sensational."[56] The earning potential that Mozart had recognized and enjoyed upon his move to Vienna

---

49. For an elaboration on how performing artists organized their own concerts in Vienna and what this entailed logistically and financially (securing a venue, funding, publicizing, sometimes obtaining permission, distributing tickets, hiring musicians, printing program announcements, etc.), see Mary Sue Morrow, *Concert Life in Haydn's Vienna: Aspects of a Developing Musical and Social Institution* (Stuyvesant, NY: Pendragon Press, 1989), 109–39.

50. Letter of 12 March 1785 in LMF, 888; MBA, 3:378.

51. Scherer, *Quarter Notes*, 60.

52. Waldoff, "Mozart and Finances," 173–74.

53. Scherer, *Quarter Notes*, 60; see letter of 12–14 July 1789 in LMF, 930.

54. Waldoff, "Mozart and Finances," 173.

55. Letter of 13 November 1777 in LMF, 369; MBA, 2:119.

56. Morrow, *Concert Life in Haydn's Vienna*, 121.

would not be sustainable long-term. Organizing one's own concerts would continue to be a risky pursuit for composers after Mozart; for example, Beethoven and Hector Berlioz often experienced great losses when organizing their own concerts.[57]

Producing new operas could also be perilous, as Leopold Mozart pointed out in a letter while rehearsals were under way for the premiere of Wolfgang's opera *Mitridate* in Milan on 26 December 1770: "As the singers are good, all will depend upon the orchestra, and ultimately upon the caprice of the audience. Thus, as in a lottery, there is a large element of luck."[58] It was common for composers to receive a single fee for opera commissions and no royalties for subsequent performances, although the composer occasionally benefited from an additional performance payment.[59] Mozart received the standard opera fee of 450 florins for *Die Entführung aus dem Serail* (1782), *Le nozze di Figaro* (1786), and *Don Giovanni* (1787 in Prague). For *Der Schauspieldirektor* (1786) and *Don Giovanni* (1788 in Vienna), he received only half this amount.[60] The fee may have been as high as 900 florins for one or more of his last three operas—*Così fan tutte* (1790), *La clemenza di Tito* (1791), and *Die Zauberflöte* (1791)—although while this figure appears in reference to the first two of these, it cannot be proven by existing payment records.[61] Mozart's Requiem, one of his final works, was commissioned in 1791 for 225 florins.

Teaching

Teaching was a common way for musicians in the eighteenth century to earn extra income; Bach and Mozart were particularly sought-after as music teachers. Bach had at least eighty-four private students throughout his career, of which seventy-one were in Leipzig. Records are limited, but we know that in Weimar, Bach was at least twice

---

57. Scherer, *Quarter Notes*, 60–61.

58. Letter of 8 December 1770 in LMF, 173–74; MBA, 1:407–8.

59. Waldoff, "Mozart and Finances," 174. Documentation shows that Mozart received the proceeds for subsequent performances of *Don Giovanni* and *Die Zauberflöte*; see Dexter Edge, "Mozart Is Awarded the Third Receipts from *Die Zauberflöte*" (5 Oct. 1791)," in *Mozart: New Documents*, ed. Dexter Edge and David Black, https://sites.google.com/site/mozartdocuments/documents/.

60. See a list of Mozart's income in Moore, "Mozart in the Market-Place," 21. According to Ian Woodfield, *The Vienna Don Giovanni* (Woodbridge, UK: Boydell Press, 2010), 41, receiving a fee for a work that had been premiered elsewhere would have been exceptional.

61. See Waldoff, "Mozart and Finances," 174; Dexter Edge, "Mozart's Fee for *Così fan tutte*," *Journal of the Royal Musical Association* 116, no. 2 (1991): 211–35; Andrew Steptoe, "Mozart, Mesmer, and 'Così Fan Tutte,'" *Music & Letters* 67, no. 3 (1986): 248–55.

remunerated for lessons in the form of firewood[62] and his student Philipp David Kräuter paid 80 thaler per year (1711–13) for board and tuition, which had been negotiated down from 100 thaler.[63] In 1732, the father of one of Bach's students, Christian Heinrich Gräbner, wrote that lessons with Bach had represented a significant cost for him.[64] Finally, a clavier lesson with Bach had cost six thaler in 1747.[65] According to Talle, the average rate for private keyboard lessons at the time was two or three groschen per hour,[66] so Bach's success in attracting a large number of students, some paying a rate much higher than average, meant that he could have earned significant supplemental income from this activity. Bach's relationship with his students proved to be productive beyond teaching, too, as students or former students were involved in engraving, printing, and circulating his music.[67]

Mozart particularly relied on income from teaching during his first years in Vienna, during which time he was teaching three to four students each day and charging twenty-seven florins for twelve lessons a month.[68] This achieved his goal of having a few well-paying students, including members of the nobility.[69] Relatively little additional information is available about his teaching, although he did seek more students later in his lifetime, writing to Michael Puchberg on or before 17 May 1790, "PS.—I now have two pupils and should very much like to raise the number to eight. Do your best to spread the news that I am willing to give lessons."[70] However, on 7 February 1778, he had indicated in a letter to his father that he saw his role as a teacher as secondary to his other occupations:

62. "2 fl. 6 gr. in the form of 1 cord of timber" (28 July 1711) and "1 fl. 6 gr. in the form of ½ cord" (25 February 1712) from Duke Ernst August, for clavier lessons for his page, Adam Friedrich Wilhelm von Jagemann; NBR, 64, no. 43; BDOK 2:44, no. 53.

63. NBR, 318–19, no. 312; BDOK 2:46–47, no. 58, BDOK 5:116–19, 274, nos. B 53a, B 53b, B 53c, B 54a, B 53ba.

64. BDOK 2:228–29, no. 319.

65. For Eugen Wenzel, Count of Wrbna; NBR, 230, no. 250; BDOK 5:108, no. A 135a.

66. Talle, *Beyond Bach*, 219.

67. Heber, *Bach's Material and Spiritual Treasures*, 46–52.

68. See letter of 16 June 1781 in LMF, 744–75; MBA, 3:131; and letter of 23 January 1782, LMF, 795; MBA, 3:195. See also Carl Bär, "Mozarts Schülerkreis," *Acta Mozartiana* 11 (1964): 58–64; and Adeline Mueller, "Learning and Teaching," in *Mozart in Context*, ed. Keefe, 10–18.

69. See letter of 26 May 1781 in LMF, 736; MBA, 3:121.

70. LMF, 939; MBA, 4:108.

I will gladly give lessons as a favour, particularly when I see that my pupil has talent, inclination and anxiety to learn; but to be obliged to go to a house at a certain hour—or to have to wait at home for a pupil—is what I cannot do, no matter how much money it may bring me in. I find it impossible, so must leave it to those who can do nothing else but play the clavier. I am a composer and was born to be a Kapellmeister. I neither can nor ought to bury the talent for composition with which God in his goodness has so richly endowed me.[71]

While Bach and Mozart could charge higher fees from wealthy students, variation in their rates indicate that they sometimes reduced them for students with modest means, which was a common practice at the time.[72] Mozart was willing to give lessons while in Mannheim in 1777 in exchange for accommodation and meals.[73] Later Mozart accommodated and taught nine-year-old Johann Nepomuk Hummel for two years (1786–88) at no charge, based on the talent and potential Mozart recognized when the boy's father brought him to audition.[74] Other accounts suggest that teaching extended beyond a duty for Mozart; on occasion he composed for or with his students, had a close and friendly relationship with his English pupil Thomas Attwood, and expressed enthusiasm for teaching Franziska von Jacquin.[75] His well-paying students were indeed a financial asset: taking into consideration summer vacations and assuming an average of four students per year, Waldoff estimates that Mozart could have earned around 600–800 florins per year from private teaching.[76]

Music Publishing

At the time of Bach's relocation to Leipzig in 1723, the practice of engraving and printing music manuscripts was only starting to develop; it was more common for composers to distribute and sell handwritten copies of their works. Bach relied on book publishers based in Leipzig or others who frequented the city during its book fairs

71. *LMF*, 468; *MBA*, 2:264.

72. Scherer, *Quarter Notes*, 64–65.

73. See Mueller, "Learning and Teaching," 15; Ruth Halliwell, *The Mozart Family: Four Lives in a Social Context* (Oxford: Oxford University Press, 1998), 261 and 271.

74. Mark Kroll, *Johann Nepomuk Hummel: A Musician's Life and World* (Lanham, MD: Rowman & Littlefield, 2007), 11–13.

75. Mueller, "Learning and Teaching," 16–17; Daniel Heartz, "Thomas Attwood's Lessons in Composition with Mozart," *Proceedings of the Royal Musical Association* 100 (1973–74): 175–83; Erich Hertzmann, "Mozart and Attwood," *JAMS* 12 (1959): 178–84; and Edward Klorman, *Mozart's Music of Friends: Social Interplay in the Chamber Works* (Cambridge: Cambridge University Press, 2016), 269–71.

76. Waldoff, "Mozart and Finances," 172.

after he initiated the publication of his own music compositions in 1726. Initially, he printed just one or two Partitas from the *Clavierübung* collection at a time, paying for the prints himself, and indicating on the cover pages that they were published by the author.[77] Surviving information is too limited to calculate his potential profits from this venture. We know only that the *Clavierübung* III (1739) sold for 3 thaler and the *Musikalisches Opfer* (1747) for one thaler.[78] He advertised his prints locally and sold them on commission through colleagues in Dresden, Berlin, Halle, Lüneburg, Brunswick, Nuremberg, and Augsburg.[79] Nevertheless, the list of prints that appeared during Bach's lifetime is relatively short; in addition to the four parts of the *Clavierübung* and the *Musikalisches Opfer*, these include the Canonic Variations on "Vom Himmel hoch" (1747–48) and the "Schübler Chorales" (1747–48).[80]

Mozart saw considerably more of his compositions in print; during his lifetime, a total of 130 were published, and most of these during his Vienna years.[81] Leopold Mozart expressed his admiration for C. P. E. Bach's publications when he wrote to J. G. I. Breitkopf on 6 October 1775 to inquire about printing possibilities:

> As I decided some time ago to have some of my son's compositions printed, I should like you to let me know as soon as possible whether you would like to publish some of them ... perhaps you would like to print clavier sonatas in the same style as those of Carl Philipp Emanuel Bach "mit veränderten Reprisen"? ... I shall be very grateful if you will send me a list of all the works of Carl Philipp Emanuel Bach which you can supply.[82]

---

77. BDOK I: 224–25, 227, 230–32, 236–37, nos. 156, 159, 162, 164, 165, 168, 169. Although *Clavierübung* I and III were self-published, *Clavierübung* II was issued by Christoph Weigel Jr. of Nuremburg. See also Christoph Wolff, *Bach's Musical Universe: The Composer and His Work* (New York: W. W. Norton, 2020), 152–91.

78. NBR, 229, 333, nos. 248, 333; BDOK 2:369–70, 386–87, nos. 455, 456, 482; 3:656, no. 558a. *Clavierübung* I had probably at some point sold for three thaler, since C. P. E. Bach indicated in 1774 that parts I and III had formerly sold together for six thaler; 3:277, no. 792. It also appears that one individual Partita from *Clavierübung* I was purchased for twelve groschen and then resold in 1735 for eight groschen; 2:255–56, no. 361.

79. NBR, 229, no. 248; 2:169, no. 224; 3:656, no 558a.

80. NBR, 223, 226, nos. 238, 243; 1:240, 244–46, nos. 172, 175, 176.

81. Simon P. Keefe and Cliff Eisen, *The Cambridge Mozart Encyclopedia* (Cambridge: Cambridge University Press, 2006), 487; see also Volkmar Braunbehrens, *Mozart in Vienna*, trans. Timothy Bell (New York: Grove Weidenfeld, 1991), 135.

82. LMF, 265; MBA, 1:527.

Mozart later submitted his works to several local music publishers in Vienna and, like Bach, was well situated for music publication, especially since the industry was growing and becoming more profitable in Vienna during his time.[83] Only one record of payment for a publication survives, indicating 450 florins (100 ducats) for the "Haydn Quartets" published by Antaria in Vienna in 1785, although it cannot be assumed that this was a consistent payment amount.[84] Mozart also attempted to set up the sale of manuscript copies of three string quintets by way of various subscription schemes, but this attempt was unsuccessful.[85] Based on the standard rates of the Viennese firms and Mozart's known publications, Maynard Solomon calculates that Mozart's fees could have ranged from 60 florins in 1783 to 900 florins in 1785, with a yearly average closer to 200–300 florins.[86]

Whereas printed music was a rare commodity in Germany before 1750, "publishers were the most public purchasers of music in late eighteenth-century Germany, Paris, London, and Vienna."[87] Yet the challenge of dividing profits between copyist, publisher, and composer was not easily resolved as the business grew, especially since composers were not yet protected by copyright laws. In 1770 Leopold Mozart wrote to his wife from Milan concerning their son's opera *Mitridate*: "The copyist is absolutely delighted, which is a good omen in Italy, where, if the music is a success, the copyist by selling the arias sometimes makes more money than the Kapellmeister does by his composition."[88] In 1782 Wolfgang Mozart was grateful when a baron purchased a copy of *Die Entführung aus dem Serail* directly from him rather than from a copyist.[89] During Mozart's time, copyists and unauthorized publishers were regularly involved

---

83. Rupert Ridgewell, "Inside a Viennese *Kunsthandlung*: Artaria in 1784," in *Consuming Music: Individuals, Institutions, Communities, 1730–1830*, ed. Emily H. Green and Catherine Mayes (Rochester, NY: University of Rochester Press, 2017), 29–61.

84. Dedicated on 1 September 1785; in *MDB*, 250; *MDL*, 220; see also Leopold's letter of 22 January 1785 in *LMF*, 885; *MBA*, 3:368. Rupert Ridgewell suggests that in 1787 Artaria paid Mozart in advance for six piano trios and twelve songs, which Mozart failed to complete. See Ridgewell, "Mozart's Publishing Plans with Artaria in 1787: New Archival Evidence," *Music & Letters* 83, no. 1 (2002): 30–74.

85. Simon P. Keefe, *Mozart in Vienna: The Final Decade* (Cambridge: Cambridge University Press, 2017), 449.

86. Solomon, *Mozart*, 525–26.

87. Emily H. Green, "Music's First Consumers: Publishers in the Late Eighteenth Century," in *Consuming Music*, ed. Green and Mayes, 13–28, esp. 24.

88. Letter of 15 December 1770 in *LMF*, 174; *MBA*, 1:408.

89. Letter of 5 October 1782 in *LMF*, 825–26; *MBA*, 3:236.

in the piracy of manuscripts throughout Europe. Mozart tried to control this impingement upon his rights by having copies made under his supervision at home.[90]

In addition to these activities common to Bach and Mozart, Bach operated a small business in Leipzig where he sold copies of his own publications and works by his sons, students, and colleagues, as well as a manuscript copying and rental service. He furthermore oversaw a number of instrument rentals and sales.[91] Interesting in this comparison is the difference in how each composer took financial risk—for Bach, it meant paying for his own prints and distributing them himself, while Mozart organized many of his own concerts and relied on generous patrons. But how did these efforts ultimately turn out for Bach and Mozart?

Financial Outcomes

Various attempts have been made to estimate what Bach may have actually earned, although it is impossible to come up with conclusive figures. The only record of his total salary in Leipzig is Bach's own estimation of "about 700 thaler" in his letter to Erdmann in 1730. Siegbert Rampe estimates overall annual earnings (salary plus freelance activities) of up to 2,000 thaler for Bach in Leipzig.[92] Eberhard Spree, in his dissertation about Anna Magdalena published in 2019, suggests that Bach must have been earning closer to 1,400 thaler per year by the end of his life.[93] While these figures are informed guesses at best, it is clear that Bach earned considerably more in Leipzig than the often-quoted amount of 700 thaler.[94]

Mozart borrowed money from his fellow Mason, Michael Puchberg, at least sixteen times from 1788 to 1791, totaling around 1,450 florins.[95] There is plenty of speculation about why Mozart found himself in financial need even though he seems to have experienced prosperity during certain periods. Uwe Krämer suggested in 1976 that

---

90. Letter of 20 February 1784 in LMF, 868; MBA, 3:302, and letter of 15 May 1784 in LMF, 876–77; MBA, 3:313–14. For more on this topic, see F. M. Scherer, "The Emergence of Musical Copyright in Europe from 1709 to 1850" (Harvard Kennedy School Faculty Research Working Paper Series RWPOS-052, October 2008).

91. Wolff, *The Learned Musician*, 412.

92. *Bachs Welt*, ed. Rampe, 138–46.

93. Eberhard Spree, *Die verwitwete Frau Capellmeisterin Bach: Studie über die Verteilung des Nachlasses von Johann Sebastian Bach* (Altenburg: Reinhold, 2019), 47–48.

94. See Heber, *Bach's Material and Spiritual Treasures*, 57–61.

95. Moore, "Mozart in the Market-Place," 18–20; for details on the requested amounts and money received, see chart in Waldoff, "Mozart and Finances," 178–79.

Mozart lost much of his money to gambling.[96] Carl Bär, two years later, refuted this claim and came up with a figure of 11,000 florins in expenses from 1785 to 1791, concluding that a deficit was caused by high expenditures.[97] In Moore's assessment of Mozart's estate in comparison to his contemporaries, she concludes, "Mozart's estate appears exceptional both in its fine possessions and in its huge debt, a likely result of a period of very high income followed by several years of considerably reduced income."[98] Solomon calculated Mozart's known and potential income based on comparable fees for his contemporaries, which results in an average yearly range of 3,672 to 5,672 florins.[99] Waldoff more recently came to a similar appraisal of 4,000 florins of annual income during Mozart's most active years as a performer, through 1786.[100]

Speculation aside, there were clear external and personal factors that contributed to Mozart's precarious financial situation in the late 1780s. The concert scene in Vienna was changing and limiting performance opportunities, the Turkish war brought about economic difficulties, and the emperor's death halted concerts during Lent in 1790.[101] Mozart's declining health in later years, medical bills for him and his wife Constanze, and a lawsuit shortly before his death would have likewise contributed to his financial concerns.[102] Nevertheless, as elaborated by Christoph Wolff, Mozart remained relatively optimistic about his future even during these difficult times, and his requests for loans were intended to bridge the way to better times.[103] Alongside his plea for financial aid in one of his letters to Puchberg in 1790, Mozart anticipates that the help could influence his future success, writing, "I now stand at the threshold

96. Uwe Krämer, "Wer hat Mozart verhungern lassen?" *Musica* 30, no. 3 (1976): 203–11. See also Andrew Steptoe, "Mozart and Poverty: A Re-examination of the Evidence," *Musical Times* 125 (1984): 196–201.

97. Carl Bär, "Er war . . . kein guter Wirth: Eine Studie über Mozart's Verhältnis zum Geld," *Acta Mozartiana*, 25, no. 1 (1978): 30–53, esp. 47. For more on medical expenses during the last years of Mozart's life, see Günther G. Bauer, *Mozart: Geld, Ruhm und Ehre* (Bad Honnef: K. H. Bock, 2009), 245–58.

98. Moore, "Mozart in the Market-Place," 37.

99. Solomon, *Mozart*, 522–23.

100. Waldoff, "Mozart and Finances," 175.

101. Waldoff, "Mozart and Finances," 175–76.

102. Mozart was sued by Count Lichnowsky for 1,435 florins and 32 kreuzer, although the lawsuit was apparently dropped after Mozart's death; Waldoff, "Mozart and Finances," 177; Keefe, *Mozart in Vienna*, 545–46. Peter Hoyt's theory is reported in Daniel J. Wakin, "Scholar Has Theory on Mozart the Debtor," *New York Times*, 28 November 2010, https://www.nytimes.com/2010/11/29/arts/music/29mozart.html.

103. Wolff, *Mozart at the Gateway*, 1–8, 28–32.

of my fortune" and "my whole future happiness is in your hands."[104] Along with the same letter, Mozart sent Puchberg a Handel biography by John Mainwaring. Wolff interprets the significance of this gift as an indication of Mozart's anticipation for what was to come:

> Above all, this eloquent little gift illuminates the composer's strong awareness of his musical net worth, his self-confidence, his forward-looking attitude, and above all, what he generally meant by the kind of fortune he could reasonably count on: fame and wealth. This was not mere wishful thinking on his part, for indeed, both came— the first more quickly than the second. But the sole beneficiary was to be his widow, Constanze, who survived the composer by more than a half-century and upon her death in 1842 still left her two sons a major fortune of some 30,000 florins in cash, bonds, and savings accounts—all based on earnings from Mozart's music.[105]

Had he survived these difficult times and lived longer than thirty-five years of age, it appears that Mozart would have had good prospects for future financial success; one need only consider the careers of contemporaries such as Joseph Haydn to imagine what he could have achieved.[106]

Conclusion

This overview has illustrated how Bach and Mozart pursued freelance work amid the challenges and opportunities that composers faced during the eighteenth century. Although they emerged from contrasting backgrounds, Bach and Mozart both ended up in affluent European cities, which not only confronted them with high living expenses, but also brought rewarding opportunities to their doorsteps, such as wealthy students and local opportunities to publish their compositions (engravers and printers in Leipzig and music publishers in Vienna). As performers, Bach was paid up to 230 thaler (including expenses) for a guest performance while Mozart apparently made a profit of 559 gulden for a public concert and had sales of up to 2,025 florins for a subscription concert series. Bach and Mozart both displayed generosity as teachers, adjusting their rates based on students' economic situations, but also benefitted from above-average fees from their wealthier apprentices. Both composers pursued publishing their own music, but Mozart saw significantly more of his compositions in print during his lifetime—130 compared to Bach's 16 prints (counting the individual partitas of the *Clavierübung* I separately).

104. Letter from the end of March or beginning of April 1790 in LMF, 936; MBA, 4:104. Quoted in Wolff, *Mozart at the Gateway*, 6.

105. Wolff, *Mozart at the Gateway*, 8.

106. Wolff, *Mozart at the Gateway*, 32.

If the informed speculations about their total earnings are accurate, Bach made up to 1,400 or possibly even 2,000 thaler per year, while Mozart may have averaged 4,000 florins during his most productive years with a potential high of 5,672 florins. This means that both of them would have achieved an economic status comparable to upper-middle-class members of society, such as the better-paid university professors and clergy members. Regardless of the shifting perspectives on how much or how little Bach and Mozart earned, it is clear that their respective financial situations were neither ideal nor unsuccessful, but rather representative of a journey in unstable times that entailed many ups and downs.

Future comparative studies of both prominent and more ordinary musicians from the eighteenth century would continue to fill the gaps left by insufficient documentation on the two composers highlighted here. Even though Bach and Mozart may represent an obvious starting point, the picture could be broadened, for example, with further associations between the freelance activities of musicians in other contexts, such as Telemann in Hamburg and Haydn in London.

Freelancing certainly offered musicians a degree of artistic freedom and financial earning potential, but even for the most celebrated composers from the eighteenth century, it was accompanied by personal financial risk. Similar uncertainties continue to confront freelance musicians today and, like Bach and Mozart, many rely on teaching as a form of regular income. However, while freelance musicians in European countries may now benefit from health insurance, royalties for publications and recordings, and often governmental subsidies, none of these aids were in place when Bach and Mozart, along with many of their contemporaries, pursued independent work. Neither of these composers was "poor," but one may be more impressed by their *pursuit* of wealth through their innovative undertakings than by the monetary wealth they actually obtained. Despite their struggles and frustrations on a financial level, Bach and Mozart produced an abundance of compositions that ironically continue even today to contribute to money-making opportunities for performers, teachers, publishers, and scholars.

Johann Christian Bach's German Heritage

Stephen Roe

In memory of Helmut Nanz (1943–2020)

Johann Christian Bach had the shortest life of the four great musical sons of Johann Sebastian, but his was the most eventful and glittering. Unlike his brothers, who seldom strayed beyond German boundaries, Christian strode the royal courts of London, Paris, Berlin, and Mannheim and many minor palaces in Italy. He probably earned more money in his heyday in London than the accumulated income of his brothers, though his bank accounts were depleted at his death in 1782. In London he was lionized by the queen and was paid more than most musicians in the city.[1] His musical travels took him all over Europe, from Berlin to Bath, from Amsterdam to Naples. His music was printed in the major centers of European music publishing, and just as frequently pirated. His manuscripts are found everywhere on the continent, even on the Iberian Peninsula, a region usually impervious to German music in the eighteenth century. Literally and figuratively, he moved further away from his father than any of the Bach children, converting to Roman Catholicism in the late 1750s, and retaining his new faith even in London, where it would have been easier to renounce it. The range of his compositions exceeds that of his brothers, who wrote no operas: he set texts in four modern languages, all of which he spoke and understood well. The variety of his musical experiences rivals George Frideric Handel's, whose music Christian revered and performed in London, and whose influence on him has yet to be fully assessed. As with Handel, Bach's work is grounded in his earliest musical training in Germany, notably Leipzig and Berlin. Also like Handel, his German musical outlook was fundamentally altered by his years in Italy, where contact with Italian opera at its source revitalized and transformed his musical style.

1. Bach's two known bank accounts, the first his personal account, the second containing newly discovered details of the Bach-Abel concert finances between 1773 and 1775, are discussed in my forthcoming book, *J. C. Bach at Work: A Descriptive Catalogue of the Autograph Music Manuscripts, Letters, Documents, Bank Accounts, and Ephemera.*

This brief survey of Johann Christian's earliest years aims to examine his primary musical experiences as a German composer in Germany and to investigate his family heritage. Using new or little-known documents and important musical autographs, I reveal that his absorption in the music of his father and half-brother Carl Philipp Emanuel was the basis of his earliest compositions and underpinned his later international style.

From his birth in Leipzig in 1735, Johann Christian Bach's earliest years were bounded by St. Thomas's, the church, school, and churchyard. The Bach family lived in an apartment in the Thomasschule, adjacent to the church. Though the older half-brothers Wilhelm Friedemann Bach, Carl Philipp Emanuel, and Johann Gottfried Bernhard had left home, the apartment was nevertheless full.[2] The younger inhabitants included Bach's daughter from his first marriage, Catharina Dorothea (b. 1708); Gottfried Heinrich (b. 1724), who was dependent on others to support him; Elisabeth Juliana Frederika (b. 1726), until her marriage to Johann Christoph Altnikol in 1749; Johann Christoph Friedrich (b. 1732); and the two youngest surviving daughters Johanna Carolina (b. 1737) and Regina Susanna (b. 1742). In addition, there were relatives, pupils, and other houseguests. This was an intense, musical home, pulsating with the sounds of rehearsals, music lessons, and the noise of the choirs, organs, and other instruments in the church, with the hours punctuated by the bells of the Thomaskirche.

Nothing is known about his schooling. Johann Christian does not appear on the roster of boys in the Thomasschule, but it is likely that he attended as an *externus*. He was well educated and intellectually gifted, to judge by his later interests in art and letters and his association with some of the greatest minds of his age in Berlin, Paris, and London. His training in Latin, and probably Greek and Hebrew, must date from these early years. He probably also sang at home and in the church choir, participating fully in the treasury of great music that his father provided in the last two decades of his life.

In this rich atmosphere Christian Bach began his musical studies. While Johann Sebastian probably supervised Christian's training, it is generally believed that day-to-day tuition was allotted to one of Sebastian's pupils. Some have suggested Altnikol or Johann Elias Bach, but a more likely candidate is Johann Nathanael Bammler (1722–84), a pupil at the Thomasschule from 1737 and in the later 1740s a musician who deputized for Sebastian at the Thomaskirche. A manuscript of five of the English Suites in Bammler's hand survives in Berlin. Some of the title pages have ownership inscriptions or annotations by Christian Bach, one being entirely in his hand (in D-B, N. Mus. ms. 365). Johann Christian assisted Bammler in preparing the scores and probably used them for practice and performance. The copying is informal, with abundant corrections and alterations. They seem hurriedly produced, the type of score

---

2. See Mark W. Knoll, "Some Reflections on Bach's Family," in *The Sons of Bach: Essays in Honor of Elias N. Kulukundis*, ed. Peter Wollny and Stephen Roe (Ann Arbor, MI: Steglein, 2016), 270–88.

a teacher might prepare for a pupil. The first suite has the added words "fait pour les Anglois" on the title page in an unknown, juvenile hand. This is the earliest known source to include any reference to the common title of these works, suggesting the term "English Suites" has some basis in fact. While it is tempting to attribute these words to Christian, the additions are in a hand that cannot be ascribed to him with any certainty. The mystery of the English Suites continues.

This manuscript, which presumably once contained all six suites, can be dated to about 1747 or 1748. These are by no means works for beginners and must represent an advanced stage in J. C. Bach's musical training. It is naturally assumed that he would have begun his keyboard studies with simple dances, minuets, polonaises, and marches, some of which are collected together in *Anna Magdalenas Clavier-Büchlein* of 1725 (in D-B, Mus. ms. Bach P 225). There have been a couple of attempts to find Christian's handwriting among the several unidentified scripts in this important collection. The "March in F" has been assigned to him by Hans-Joachim Schulze and Ernest Warburton,[3] but Peter Wollny has conclusively debunked this attribution.[4] In fact, J. C. Bach's only contribution has been completely overlooked until recently.[5] The words "Aria di G[i]ovannini" on the title page of the song "Willst du dein Hertz mir schenken" (BWV 518) are in J. C. Bach's hand. This song is usually attributed to an obscure musician called Giovannini, possibly the comte de Saint Germain, who performed in Germany around 1740 and may have been around later. The music is in an unknown hand, possibly Giovannini himself; it is certainly someone unused to German *Schrift*.

When Johann Christian wrote those words in his mother's book is unclear, but the inscription probably dates from toward the end of his years in Leipzig, between 1748 and 1750, when he did most of his secretarial and copying work for his father. The aria attracted attention early on. One of the first owners, Carl Friedrich Zelter, drafted a note on the endpapers of the manuscript itself, suggesting that Giovannini was Johann Sebastian himself.[6] This can be discounted and so can any attribution to Johann Christian.[7]

The *Clavier-Büchlein* presents a number of mysteries, not least the dual pagination, one of which ignores the aria, which was paginated later, probably by Carl Friedrich

---

3. Hans-Joachim Schulze, "Die Bach-Überlieferung, Pläydoyer für ein notwendiges Buch," *Beiträge zur Musikwissenschaft* 17 (1975): 48; see also Warb A 22.

4. Peter Wollny, "Tennstädt, Leipzig, Naumburg, Halle-Neuerkenntnisse zur Bach-Ueberlieferung in Mitteldeutschland," *BJ* 88 (2002): 29–60.

5. I am immensely grateful to Peter Wollny for drawing my attention to his discovery.

6. "*Giovannini* könnte Joh. S. Bachs italisirter Schäfername seyn."

7. Johann Christian's family nickname was "Christel." He was known by some in Italy as "Giovannino," but it is unlikely that Christian would have dubbed himself with this name in the plural form.

Zelter. This led some commentators to suggest that it was either an interpolation in the volume or had been cut out by Anna Magdalena and later reinstated somehow after the first pagination. However, the paper of both title and music is identical to the 1725 sections of the manuscript and is uniform throughout. The book was already bound when J. C. Bach inserted those three words, written on the only title page of the book. Given that Christian Bach's parents were notoriously sparing in their use of paper, perhaps the boy added these words unsupervised.

This small inscription opens up new vistas. Here is evidence that Johann Christian knew his mother's book, used it, and was trusted, or at least managed, to make an entry in it himself. Its musical content was seen and known by him and was part of his early musical activities. He knew or was at least aware of the Partitas in A Minor and E Minor from the first volume of the *Clavierübung* (BWV 827 and 830), the first two "French Suites" (BWV 812 and 813), the various minuets, polonaises, arias, and chorales, the aria of the "Goldberg Variations" (BWV 988/1), and the Prelude in C Major from the first book of the *Well-Tempered Clavier* (BWV 846/1), which are included in the *Clavier-Büchlein* before Giovannini's aria, and probably all the music that followed. These works formed the bedrock of Johann Christian's initial training, underpinning his musical thinking, even after his style changed fundamentally upon contact with Italianate music at its source.

Johann Christian also knew the Partita in A Minor from another source. He owned a copy of the rare first printing (1727), which he signed with his initials and dated 1748 (in A-Wn, Hoboken J. S. Bach 50). It is a poorly printed copy: the impressions are not square to the page; the inking is imperfect with offsetting and inkblots. Probably unsellable, it was nevertheless deemed usable within the family, and was acquired by Christian. The only other surviving example of this issue, once owned by Johannes Brahms and now in the British Library (GB-Lbl, K.10 a.30), is much better, even handsomely printed, though the quality of engraving still leaves something to be desired.

Although the A Minor partita is not the most technically challenging of Sebastian's keyboard works, it says much for the technique of the thirteen- or fourteen-year-old Johann Christian to be able to attempt it. There are few accounts of his keyboard playing. When J. C. Bach passed through Rome in 1756, the composer Girolamo Chiti (1679–1759), wrote to Padre Martini that Bach performed in the manner of the "Gran Sassone," meaning Handel.[8] Chiti was old enough to have heard Handel in Italy and knew what he was talking about. Chiti also writes that Christian played more in a Prussian rather than Saxon style. In an unknown and unpublished account, the Dessau flautist Georg Kottowski, who was in London in the late 1750s and early 1760s, and was

---

8. Letter to Martini, 20 November 1756, I-Bc, I.006.119; summary in Ann Schnoebelen, *Padre Martini's Collection of Letters in the Civico Museo Bibliografico Musicale in Bologna* (New York: Pendragon, 1979), 207, no. 1641.

a friend and correspondent of Bach, also speaks of him in the same breath as Handel.[9] There is every reason to believe that Johann Christian's keyboard skills, at least in his earliest years, were the equal of all his musical brothers. In later life, particularly his years in London, keyboard playing formed the main element of Bach's practical career, as a performer, composer, and teacher. He was the leading exponent at the court and was a wholehearted devotee of the new piano, about which he proselytized, dispatching instruments to friends around Europe.[10] Yet Charles Burney, who only knew Bach in London, is qualified about Christian's keyboard expertise. In his *General History of Music*, he describes Bach's early excellent playing but, citing the composer himself, states that he played the keyboard little in Italy, except for accompanying singers. "When he arrived in England, his style of playing was so much admired, that he recovered many of the losses his hand had sustained by disuse, and by being constantly cramped and crippled by the pen; but he never was able to reinstate it with force and readiness sufficient for great difficulties."[11] At the height of his career in England, Bach was playing the keyboard at court and in the concert hall several times a week, as well as earning money by teaching. It is difficult to imagine that he could retain his popularity for so long if the early brilliance of his German years had greatly diminished.

Christian Bach's career as a composer really began when he moved to Berlin in 1750. A few modest works can be dated to Leipzig, such as the simple minuets and polonaises for harpsichord, similar to those in Anna Magdalena's book. These survive in a manuscript compendium (in D-B, Mus. ms. Bach P 672) of Bach family works, copied by Emanuel Bach's Hamburg copyist Michel. Christian's first dated autograph (23 October 1748), now lost, an album leaf, is a transcription for keyboard of the Polonaise from his father's Second Orchestral Suite, transposed to D minor.[12] Fortunately, a photograph of this first dateable manuscript exists (see figure 4.1). Johann Christian attempts vaingloriously and ineffectively to recall the transcription, which also survives in Michel's album from Hamburg. Johann Christian's effort is full of errors and mistakes. He would surely have garnered a paternal rebuke for his defective musical memory and for his faulty Latin.

When his sons approached their teenage years, Johann Sebastian began to use them as copyists and amanuenses. The teenage Johann Christoph Friedrich, who was three

9. See J. C. Bach's letter to Kottowski, dated 26 June 1764, in D-DElsa, Z 44, A 12b 4 No. 1, Bl. 19; inaccurately transcribed in Warburton, 48/2, 541. Kottowski's autobiographical statement is in D-DElsa, Z 44, A 12b 4 No. 1a, Bl. 3.

10. Bach sent pianos to the French pianists Madame Brillon and Angélique, daughter of Denis Diderot. Four pianos signed by Bach are known.

11. Charles Burney, *A General History of Music and Musicians*, 4 vols. (London, 1776–89), 4:482.

12. Reproduced in Hans-Joachim Schulze, "Frühe Schriftzeugnisse der beiden jüngsten Bach-Söhne," *BJ* 53–54 (1963–64): 61–69.

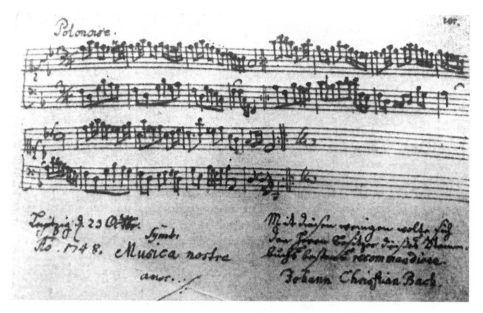

Figure 4.1. Album leaf (now lost) signed by J. C. Bach, with the Polonaise
of J. S. Bach's Second Orchestral Suite. Reproduced from a photograph
courtesy of the Bach-Archiv Leipzig.

years older than Johann Christian, was one of the principal copyists of the orchestral
parts of the final version of the *St. John Passion* (1749/50), working alongside Bammler. Christian was not entrusted with major copying projects for his father, tending
to be used only when time was short and all hands required. Thus, his contributions
are found in manuscripts where there are many other scribes. He also worked closely
with Bammler on the parts of the *St. John Passion* (in D-B, Mus. ms. Bach St 111), a
further indication perhaps of the mentor/pupil relationship. Christian contributed to
these parts at a late stage, his contributions often appearing on added leaves. In this
page from the "Traversière Primo" (see figure 4.2), there are three hands: the upper
two lines, containing the recitative and first measure of the aria "Zerfliesse" are in
the late hand of Johann Sebastian. Johann Christian takes over in measure 2, possibly
using the same ink and pen as his father, and writes until the end of the sixth line. At
the beginning of the seventh line, with the change of clef, Bammler takes over briefly.
Christian continues from line 8 for the remainder of the aria. This demonstrates the
metaphorical and actual closeness of Christian Bach and Bammler.

Johann Christian was a copyist for his father from about 1748. His hand is found
in the final revision of the wedding cantata *Dem Gerechten muss das Licht*, BWV 195
(1748–49; in D-B, Mus. ms. Bach St 12), and the festive *Wir danken Dir, Gott*, BWV 29,
where he transcribes a basso continuo part (in D-B, Mus. ms. Bach 106). Neither work
is written for one of the great cycles of cantatas for the Sundays of the year but are

Figure 4.2. "Traversière Primo" part in the hands of J. S. Bach, J. C. Bach, and J. N. Bammler from the *St. John Passion*, BWV 245. Courtesy of D-B, Mus. ms. Bach St 111.

discrete pieces for special events. *Wir danken dir, Gott,* BWV 29, contains a version of the "Gratias agimas"/"Agnus Dei" from the Mass in B Minor, which Bach was completing at the time the cantata was revived. Thus, this extraordinary music was known to the young Johann Christian. The cantata also makes use of the opening movement of the Violin Partita in E Major in the Sinfonia, arranged as an organ concerto. An obligato organ also appears in the aria "Hallelujah, Stark und Macht." Perhaps this was the inspiration for Johann Christian in the solo organ in two movements of his *Confitebor,* Warb E 16, composed in Milan in 1759, which the composer may have performed himself. Christoph Wolff suggests Christian may also have been an instrumentalist in *Wir danken dir, Gott.*[13] But, if so, Christian is unlikely to have used the continuo part that he copied, as it is not transposed and unfigured, and more likely meant for a string bass instrument than for keyboard.

Christian also participated in the copying of an entire motet, "Herr, nun lässest du deinen Diener in Frieden fahren," by Johann Christoph Bach (in D-B, Mus. ms. Bach P 4/2), whose music Johann Sebastian revered. One might imagine that there would be no connection between Johann Christoph and Johann Christian Bach, apart from the coincidence of their initials, but surprisingly, when writing church music under Padre Martini, the somewhat stodgy *Invitatorio,* with its cantus firmus in the bass, gives more than a passing nod to his distinguished ancient forebear.

The death of Johann Sebastian in July 1750, though anticipated, was nevertheless devasting, causing the family to split, Anna Magdalena having to downsize drastically, selling some manuscripts to the Thomaskirche and probably losing control of the remainder to her stepsons. When J. C. Bach left Leipzig for Berlin, probably in December 1750, he took with him a knowledge of the French and English Suites, the keyboard Partitas, the *St. John Passion,* at least two cantatas, and probably the two- and three-part Inventions and both books of the *Well-Tempered.* He also knew the *Streit zwischen Phöbus und Pan,* BWV 201, for he helped in the transcription of the revised libretto (in D-B, Mus. ms. Bach P 175), and probably a few concertos and orchestral works. He inherited at least two autographs of organ music by his father, the Prelude and Fugue in B Minor, BWV 544, which survives (in US-NYpm, Lehman Deposit B 1184, p. 898), bearing Christian's family nickname "Christel" in Anna Magdalena's hand; and the lost manuscript of the Toccata in E Major, BWV 566, also apparently marked with the same soubriquet.[14]

13. Christoph Wolff, *Johann Sebastian Bach: The Learned Musician* (New York: W. W. Norton, 2000), 444–45.

14. See the manuscript copy of a transcription in C major by J. P. Kellner in D-B, Mus. ms. Bach P 286/3, which contains an inscription by Johann Jakob Heinrich Westphal that refers to a lost manuscript in E Major marked "Christel."

In Leipzig, Christian figured only as a shadow against the brilliant background of his father; in Berlin he disappears almost completely. Accounts of his activities are scarce. Emanuel, who published his celebrated keyboard treatise, the *Versuch über die wahre Art das Clavier zu spielen*, in 1753, continued Christian's keyboard tuition and supervised his composing. Christian performed on the harpsichord in public and attended the premiere of Carl Heinrich Graun's *Der Tod Jesu* in early 1755.[15] Little else is known. Emanuel replaced Sebastian as his main influence. In his last years in Leipzig Christian transcribed Emanuel's Sonata in B-flat Major, Wq 62/1 (in D-B, Mus. ms. P 841), with its strong resemblance to J. S. Bach's two-part Invention in F Major, and he made at least two more copies of his half-brother's works in Berlin: the keyboard part of the Concerto in G Minor, Wq 32 (in D-B, Mus. ms. St 534), and the Sonata in E-flat, Wq 65/28 (in D-B, Mus. ms. P 776). Both works influenced Christian's emerging musical style, and indeed his own early Sonata in A-flat Major, Warb A 14, probably written in Italy, quotes from Emanuel's sonata.[16]

The most important compositions written by Christian in Berlin are six keyboard concertos. Five survive in an autograph (in D-B, Mus. ms. Bach P 390), abandoned in Berlin when he went to Italy in 1755. An autograph sketch of a sixth Concerto in F Minor clinches his authorship of a work elsewhere attributed in contemporary manuscripts to C. P. E and W. F. Bach.[17] The autographs of the five concertos date between 1753 and 1755: the paper of the manuscripts is broadly similar to that used in Wq 32 and 65/28, composed around the same time. (Both works are dated 1754 in C. P. E. Bach's *Nachlassverzeichnis*.)

The autograph shows the five concertos as "fruit of long and laborious endeavor," to adapt Mozart's words about his String Quartets for Franz Joseph Haydn. The multiple paper-types, revealing that many early drafts were discarded and replacement pages added, show that Christian worked long and hard on these works. As all were composed in Berlin on local paper, the notion that the first concerto was written in Leipzig under the supervision of Sebastian is invalid.[18]

These early works by Christian are steeped in Emanuel's musical language. They exude a seriousness and sobriety seldom found in Christian's output after Berlin. Half the movements are in minor keys, rarely used in his later concertos and symphonies. Key relationships between movements are adventurous. The concertos are longer and

15. See Ernst Ludwig Gerber, *Historisch-biographisches Lexikon der Tonkünstler*, 2 vols. (Leipzig, 1790–92), 1:83; and Friedrich Wilhelm Marpurg, *Legende einiger Musikheiligen* (Cologne, 1786), 306.

16. For further discussion of this sonata see Stephen Roe, *The Keyboard Music of J. C. Bach: Source Problems and Stylistic Development in the Solo and Ensemble Works* (New York: Garland, 1989), 157–66.

17. The sketch is found on the last page of the autograph manuscript of the Concerto in B-flat Major.

18. See Richard Maunder's introduction to CWJCB, vol 32, x.

more virtuosic than any of his mature compositions. The musical language is rich and varied, with sudden pauses, unusual, grinding harmonies, and unexpected plunges into remote tonalities. The second concerto in F Minor strongly resembles the opening of Wq 32, which Christian might have performed from the keyboard part he prepared. Emanuel's musical mannerisms predominate, not least the ending of the ritornellos in octaves, a trope reminiscent of Shakespeare ending a scene with a rhyming couplet. Stylistic fingerprints of Emanuel, such as themes that cover a fifth stepwise, sudden changes of harmony, and the use of tactical surprises with sharp juxtapositions of *forte* and *piano*, are all present. Extremes of tempo, adagios next to prestos, are never found elsewhere in Christian's output. "Presto" and "prestissimo" are seldom used again, only once in the solo keyboard music of the London era. But Johann Christian also expresses individuality here. There is a smiling quality to the faster movements, anticipating the "singing allegro" style of his later works; and sometimes a more sensuous feeling pervades the slow movements. Both these features are somewhat alien to Emanuel's aesthetic. It is too easy to think of J. C. Bach's later style as being forged exclusively in Italy. But harbingers of the Italianate manner are evident in Christian Bach's music even before he crossed the Alps.

Two other important events took place in Berlin around the time Christian went to Italy. The song "Mezendore" became his first published work,[19] and he made his first steps into a wider intellectual life. The album of the influential German publisher, Christoph Friedrich Nicolai, contains an autograph song by Bach, "Der Weise auf dem Lande," Warb H 2 (in D-B, Nachlass Nicolai II, 3) a setting of a poem by Johann Peter Uz, published in 1755, the year of composition. Nicolai was a friend and collaborator of Moses Mendelssohn; Uz was also of his circle and the presence of this song in Nicolai's album suggests that Christian was already involved in the wider intellectual milieux of the city, as he was later to be in London and Paris. He can also now be added to the roster of the first Berlin song school.

In mid-1755 Johann Christian took the momentous step of traveling to Italy. Ernst Ludwig Gerber suggests the journey was inspired by Christian's acquaintance with a group of Italian women singers in Berlin;[20] and Johann Nikolaus Forkel adds the titillating detail that he accompanied one of them to Italy.[21] Neither his traveling companions nor his route is known, though he may have journeyed via Leipzig, where

19. Song no. 12 is attributed to "Christ. Bach" in Marpurg's *Neue Lieder zum Singen beym Clavier* (Berlin, 1756). Given that J. C. Bach lived in Berlin and was personally known to Marpurg, this attribution is likely to be correct.

20. Gerber, *Historisch-biographisches Lexikon*, 1:83.

21. Johann Nikolaus Forkel, *Musikalischer Almanach für Deutschland auf das Jahr 1783* (Leipzig, 1783), 150.

his mother and sisters still lived. It is not known how long he intended to stay in Italy. The fact that he left behind the autographs of his keyboard concertos with his brother, together with a few other compositions that he never reclaimed, might indicate that he expected to return. There is almost no trace of his presence in Italy in 1755–56, save that he acquired a Milanese patron in Count Agostino Litta, an intellectual and a scientist, and a member of one of the richest families in Lombardy. And he also found a teacher in Padre Martini in Bologna.

The Bach family was not an unknown quantity to Martini, who was already acquainted with the music of Johann Sebastian and admired it. In 1750 he received a parcel of music from a friend in Fulda named Johannes Baptist Pauli.[22] This contained printed and manuscript music, some of which can be identified with sources surviving today in Martini's library, including four movements in manuscript from the Sixth Partita for keyboard and a first edition of *Das musikalische Opfer* (in I-Bc, DD 71, 73, 75, and 76). Two other important Bach sources came to Martini via another route: a manuscript of some preludes and fugues from the *Well-Tempered Clavier* in W. F. Bach's hand (in I-Bc, DD 70) and a first edition, second issue (with Marpurg's preface), of *Die Kunst der Fuge* (in I-Bc, DD 72), which is inscribed unobtrusively by C. P. E. Bach to "Herrn Benda," likely to be Johann Georg Benda, who died in the first half of 1752, before Emanuel was able to present the copy to him.[23] These items can only have come directly from the family, the obvious conduit being Johann Christian himself. If Bach brought gifts from Berlin to Padre Martini, it suggests that he always intended to have lessons with Martini and was possibly in contact with him before he left for Italy. The castrato Giovanni Tedeschi, known professionally as Amadori, was a friend and correspondent of Padre Martini. He was in Berlin in 1754–55, when he sang the title role in the premiere of Graun's *Montezuma*, and it seems likely that he was the link between Johann Christian and his revered teacher in Bologna.

Christian Bach's first works written in Italy are still hewn from the same Germanic rock as the concertos. The vast *Miserere*, Warb E 10, and *Dies irae*, Warb E 12, still display a formidable severity, which they share with the contemporary keyboard works, the Sonatas in A-flat Major, Warb A 14, and in B-flat Major, Warb A 16, and a Toccata

---

22. Martini's draft acknowledgment of receipt is written on Pauli's third surviving letter to him dated 13 February 1750. The music arrived via Piero Vanino en route to Rome. Pauli enclosed a note with the package dated 9 March 1750. The surviving letters of Pauli are at *I-Bc*. See Schnoebelen, *Padre Martini's Collection of Letters*, 474, nos. 3992–96.

23. Emanuel's dedications are often laconic and seldom effusive. But in this case, it could even be an aide-mémoire. Marpurg's preface is dated "In der Leipziger Ostermesse 1752." The second issue of *Die Kunst der Fuge* probably appeared in the second quarter of that year.

in B-flat Minor, Warb A 15. The Sonata in D Major for violin and keyboard, which Warburton thought was spurious (Warb YB 38), but the autograph manuscript tells otherwise, also retains a number of Prussian fingerprints. Immersion in Italian opera in Naples and Milan soon softened the edges of Bach's musical style, with a slowing down of the harmonic rhythms and an emphasis on balance and propriety, far from the loose structures of the Berlin concertos. Padre Martini, who acted as a sort of surrogate father to J. C. Bach, probably played a greater a role in his musical upbringing than Johann Sebastian. Martini's work on proportion in music greatly influenced Christian Bach, fundamentally altering his musical manner and guiding his career.

In later years, the German and Italian elements in Christian's music were subsumed into a more international style also influenced by English popular elements and dances, with the occasional nod to Handel and Gluck. But J. C. Bach's German heritage keeps making occasional appearances, not only in the livelier finales of the op. 17 keyboard sonatas, which seem to reference some of Sebastian's suites and partitas, but also in the Symphony in G Minor, op. 6, no. 6 (Warb C 12, composed before 1770), one of Christian's few attempts at the *Sturm und Drang* style, which reverts to the odd key juxtapositions (G minor, C minor, G minor) of the Berlin concertos. The outer movements include passages in octaves at significant structural moments, again recalling the earlier concertos. And the creepy tread of the slow movement harks back to the slow movements of C. P. E. Bach and the North German tradition. The prelude-like opening movement and the following fugue of the Sonata op. 5, no. 6 (Warb A 6) certainly owe a debt to the Bach family tradition, but the double fugue and the final gavotte also show similarities with the early sonatas of Padre Martini, which Johann Christian probably encountered in Bologna.[24] The clearest acknowledgment of the family tradition can been seen in the first movement of the accompanied sonata op. 10, no. 1 (Warb B 2, published in 1773 but probably composed some years earlier), which adapts the opening material of J. S. Bach's Prelude from the first keyboard partita, a work that undoubtedly resonated in Johann Christian's mind from his earliest years.

Bach's German core, while concealed beneath the influence of Italian opera, was never destroyed. His removal to Italy provided a new stimulus to the musical forms and ideas that he had already begun to articulate in Germany. Italian finesse and lyricism harnessed to a Germanic strength of harmony and sense of direction formed the basis of Johann Christian Bach's mature international style.

24. For further discussion, see Roe, *The Keyboard Music of J. C. Bach*, 157.

Mozart, J. C. Bach,
and the Bach Tradition

David Schulenberg

It is not fashionable, as it once was, to explain musical styles as the creations of individual composers. The biological metaphor according to which styles have single progenitors, evolving like species, is obviously imprecise; the youngest Bach son, Johann Christian, was no missing link between Johann Sebastian Bach and Wolfgang Amadeus Mozart. Nevertheless, by 1760, ten years after the death of his father, J. C. Bach was composing vocal and instrumental music whose style anticipates that of music written by Mozart a decade or two later. To some degree this music was in a generic European or Italianate style, shared with many other composers. Yet what most listeners today recognize as Mozart's style was, to a considerable degree, the invention specifically of J. C. Bach.

At issue here is not the unique style of Mozart's most profound works, such as the late quintets or the Requiem, but neither is it the generic *galant* or early Classical style of innumerable lesser contemporaries. Rather it includes certain specific features, detailed below, that can be identified in the music of first J. C. Bach and subsequently Mozart. This raises the issue of Mozart's debt to a so-called Bach tradition. The phrase "Bach tradition" occurs in multiple publications, but its precise meaning is elusive. In the popular press it often refers to present-day musicians who specialize in compositions by J. S. Bach or who have some professional connection with a venue where the latter are performed, such as the Thomaskirche in Leipzig or any number of Bach festivals. Scholars often employ the phrase in a more concrete sense, invoking its etymological root in the Latin verb *trado* (to transmit or hand down), whether in the sense of a teacher conveying knowledge to a pupil, or a composer—in particular, Bach himself— literally passing a manuscript on to an heir, or to a copyist for reproduction.[1] Naturally

---

1. For the first meaning, see, e.g., Graham Dixon, "Communicating the Bach Tradition," review of Ignace Bossuyt, *Het Weihnachts-Oratorium (BWV 248) van Johann Sebastian Bach, Early Music* 31 (2003): 290–91; for the latter sense, see, e.g., Christoph Wolff, "Bach and the Tradition of the Palestrina

it is possible for these concepts to commingle, as in discussions of Bach reception or the Bach revival. Both of these involved pupils of Bach, or copyists of his music, who also performed it and passed it on to subsequent generations. Indeed, Bach's teaching must be considered crucial to both aspects of any Bach tradition, in view of the role that the preparation of manuscript copies played in the education of young musicians in the eighteenth century.[2]

The focus here is on elements of the elder Bach's teaching and compositional style that can be traced through his sons to those composers we recognize as Classical—more specifically, from Sebastian's youngest son Johann Christian Bach to Mozart. As is well known, Mozart met J. C. Bach in London in 1764 and continued to admire the older composer until his death eighteen years later. At some point Mozart also discovered certain contrapuntal pieces by J. S. Bach, eventually making arrangements of some and echoing elements of these and other works in his own compositions. The mature Mozart's reception of Sebastian Bach was essentially a matter of integrating certain easily recognized features, especially a particular type of imitative counterpoint, into an existing personal style.[3] The younger Mozart's emulation of Christian Bach, if such it was, is less easily distinguished within his compositional development, in part because distinctive features of J. C. Bach's music are not so readily recognized today. Can one, in fact, identify unique musical parallels between compositions by J. C. Bach and Mozart, as opposed to general stylistic commonalities and the occasional thematic quotation? And do these parallels in any way reflect Christian Bach's own training and presumed familiarity with his father's music? To rephrase these questions: Does J. C. Bach's music in fact belong to a "Bach tradition," and did he transmit any part of that tradition to Mozart?

After some general considerations, I will explore possible answers to those questions within the spheres of counterpoint, symphonic writing, and instrumental color, concluding with observations of an aesthetic nature. The aim is not to find the origins or trace the development of the style of either composer. Rather, this essay has the

---

Style," in *Bach: Essays on His Life and Music* (Cambridge, MA: Harvard University Press, 1991), 84–104, in which the phrases "Palestrina tradition" and "Bach tradition" refer above all to manuscript transmission.

2. The copying of a teacher's compositions, especially those for keyboard instruments, was a fundamental part of the training of Bach's pupils—and of *their* students—as shown by the patterns of manuscript transmission traced by Hans-Joachim Schulze, *Studien zur Bach-Überlieferung im 18. Jahrhundert* (Leipzig: Peters, 1984), where the German noun *Überlieferung* is a literal translation of Latin *transmissio*.

3. Robert L. Marshall reviews nineteenth- and twentieth-century considerations of Mozart's "Bach reception" in "Bach and Mozart's Artistic Maturity," *Bach Perspectives* 3 (1998): 47–79; reprinted in Marshall, *Bach and Mozart* (Rochester, NY: University of Rochester Press, 2019), 212–37.

more limited goal of defining certain common features—including commonalities also with the music of J. S. Bach—more accurately than has been done so far. Previous investigations of the relationship between J. C. Bach and Mozart have focused on more concrete, if relatively superficial, varieties of "reception." These include Mozart's arrangement of three keyboard sonatas by Christian Bach into concertos (K 107), as well as his quotation of a theme by J. C. Bach in the Concerto in A Major, K 414 (1782), following the older composer's death earlier that year.[4] There are also Mozart's embellishments and cadenzas for two of J. C. Bach's arias (K 293e), including "Cara la dolce fiamma" from *Adriano in Siria*, which had its premiere at London in 1765 during Mozart's visit there. The existence of these examples clearly demonstrates the younger composer's fascination with music by a member of the Bach family, but it does not prove his serious engagement with a Bach tradition as defined above.

The influence of one creative artist on another is notoriously difficult to evaluate. Popular appraisals of influence tend to be based on obvious quotations or reworkings of the types just listed. Yet, as Peter Williams pointed out, a composer's most important influences might be ones from which he or she "swerves" away, purposefully *not* doing what a predecessor or contemporary has done.[5] The young Mozart—like Sebastian Bach—was capable of soaking up and recombining ideas from a diverse array of music, old as well as current. Indeed, Mozart claimed that he could write in any style,[6] and like most young musicians he initially must have learned primarily by imitation. Unlike most talented children, however, he was able almost immediately to surpass virtually everything that he heard, in original compositions ranging from little keyboard pieces to symphonies and polyphonic masses. The danger in being a fluent imitator is that one might never find a style of one's own or create anything truly distinctive. The mature Mozart's confrontation with the music of the older Bach impelled him away

4. The slow movement of the concerto quotes from the overture to *La calamita de' cuori*, also listed as Warb G27a. The same theme occurs in the little Minuet K 315a, no. 4. Mozart similarly quoted Carl Friedrich Abel in the violin sonata K 526 after the latter's death in 1787, leading Daniel Heartz to suggest that Mozart "considered his London models, Bach and Abel, to have been of equal importance to him"; see Heartz, "Abel, Christian Bach, and Gainsborough," in *Artists and Musicians: Portrait Studies from the Rococo to the Revolution*, ed. Beverly Wilcox (Ann Arbor, MI: Steglein, 2014); reprinted in *J. C. Bach*, ed. Paul Corneilson (Farnham, UK: Ashgate, 2015), 99–137, esp. 188. This may be doubted, however, if only because Abel was not a composer of the most important genre of the time, Italian opera.

5. Peter Williams, "Is There an Anxiety of Influence Discernible in J. S. Bach's *Clavierübung I?*" in *The Keyboard in Baroque Europe*, ed. Christopher Hogwood (Cambridge: Cambridge University Press, 2003), 140–56.

6. As he wrote to his father in a letter of 7 February 1778: "I can more or less adopt or imitate any kind and any style of composition." See LMF, 468; MBA, 2:265.

from the common French, Italian, and Austrian traditions to which he was exposed as a child; the question is to what degree J. C. Bach also contributed to this, and whether in doing so he was following a "Bach tradition."

J. C. Bach and the Bach Tradition?

For present purposes we might define "Bach tradition" as an approach to composition that includes substantive elements of what J. S. Bach taught his many pupils. Unfortunately, limited information survives about this.[7] For this reason the concept of a Bach tradition must remain somewhat open-ended, extending to what we can surmise about training and teaching by Sebastian's pupils, especially his second son Carl Philipp Emanuel. Sebastian's teaching as such might have been limited to the traditional topics of keyboard playing and figured bass realization. But some students would also have learned by hearing him perform and by making manuscript copies of his music. And surely a few, including his older sons, received his comments and guidance in relation to their first compositional essays. As is well known, none of the Bach sons imitated their father's style, and at least three of them went their own ways compositionally. The oldest, Wilhelm Friedemann, shared his father's interest in counterpoint, but his instrumental music consists largely of sonatas and other popular genres of the mid-eighteenth century. Emanuel Bach, while composing in the same genres, retained Sebastian's fascination with chromaticism and remote modulations while also continuing his father's practice of writing out melodic embellishment—even if the style of that embellishment was very different.[8]

It is hard to find comparable stylistic commonalities between the music of J. S. and J. C. Bach. Not only for this reason, Christian Bach is often viewed as standing apart from the Bach tradition. That he was even something of a traitor to it could be drawn not only from the obvious stylistic distinctions between his music and that of his father and older brothers, but also from his eventual conversion to Roman Catholicism.

---

7. Studies of J. S. Bach's teaching that go beyond generalities are surprisingly few; see, e.g., George B. Stauffer, "J. S. Bach as Organ Pedagogue," in *The Organist as Scholar: Essays in Memory of Russell Saunders*, ed. Kerala J. Snyder (Stuyvesant, NY: Pendragon, 1994), 25–44; and Daniel R. Melamed, "J. F. Doles's Setting of a Picander Libretto and J. S. Bach's Teaching of Vocal Composition," *Journal of Musicology* 14 (1996): 453–74.

8. For further consideration of the training and compositional styles of the two oldest Bach sons in relation to their father, see David Schulenberg, *The Music of Wilhelm Friedemann Bach* (Rochester, NY: University of Rochester Press, 2010), chap. 2; and David Schulenberg, *The Music of Carl Philipp Emanuel Bach* (Rochester, NY: University of Rochester Press, 2014), also chap. 2. Sebastian's penultimate son, Johann Christoph Friedrich Bach, seems to have begun his compositional career imitating his older half-brother Emanuel, later emulating his younger brother Christian after visiting the latter in London in 1778.

After Sebastian's death, however, his youngest son traveled with the oldest to Berlin, remaining there for about five years, living and continuing his studies with his half-brother Emanuel. If we consider the "Bach tradition" to include whatever Emanuel might have taught Christian, the meaning of the expression might be substantially broadened—although one would not wish it to become so attenuated as to lose all connection with the qualities and values of Sebastian's music.

At Berlin, Christian Bach entered the realm, musical as well as temporal, of Prussian king Friedrich II (called the Great) and of his chief composers Carl Heinrich Graun and Johann Joachim Quantz. The Berlin style was in fact a transposed Dresden style, blending what we recognize as the late Baroque manner of Antonio Vivaldi and other Venetians with *galant* elements associated especially with the "Neapolitan" style of Johann Adolph Hasse.[9] It gradually evolved into what has been called a "Berliner Klassik,"[10] reflecting an aesthetic that favored the transparent texture and clarity of expression that Quantz and other Berlin writers on music found in works of Graun and Hasse, in particular. Mozart's father Leopold, whose treatise on violin playing was published four years after Quantz's on the flute, adhered to the same aesthetic.[11] Even Emanuel Bach adopted it, to some degree, and J. C. Bach must have been inculcated in it at Berlin, if not before his arrival there. Yet any member of the Bach family working in Berlin would have felt bound to understand not only how to compose and perform *galant* music such as Graun and Quantz epitomized, but also how to give it an individual twist, to make it his own. Emanuel had learned to do this even before his arrival at Berlin in 1738, and Christian began to do so as well, as is evident in several early sonatas and concertos written largely in emulation of his brother Emanuel yet occasionally betraying other influences.[12]

---

9. On Berlin's (and also Bach's) debt to Dresden, see Mary Oleskiewicz, "Quantz and the Flute at Dresden: His Instruments, His Repertory, and Their Significance for the *Versuch* and the Bach Circle" (PhD diss., Duke University, 1998), chap. 5.

10. Christoph Henzel, *Berliner Klassik: Studien zur Graunüberlieferung im 18. Jahrhundert* (Beeskow: Ortus, 2009), especially chap. 12, "Berliner Klassik: Ein Resümee."

11. On Leopold's "rationalist aesthetic," modeled on that of Johann Christoph Gottsched and other contemporaries, see Katherine H. Walker, "Leopold Mozart, the Rationalist? Humanism and Good Taste in Eighteenth-Century Musical Thought," *Yale Journal of Music and Religion* 3 (2017): 64–84. Leopold's (and Wolfgang's) aesthetics are conveniently summarized in Thomas McPharlin Ford, "Between *Aufklärung* and *Sturm und Drang*: Leopold and Wolfgang Mozart's View of the World" (PhD diss., University of Adelaide, 2010), chap. 2; published online at https://digital.library.adelaide .edu.au/dspace/bitstream/2440/68809/8/02whole.pdf.

12. For instance, although the early keyboard concertos composed by J. C. Bach at Berlin closely resemble contemporary examples by Emanuel Bach, in certain respects they seem to follow other models, perhaps by Franz Benda, as in the preparation of the cadenza by an interrupted ritornello,

If J. C. Bach was being groomed for a future career as a royal chamber musician, following in Emanuel's footsteps, he would have learned as much of the Berlin repertory as possible. He also would have learned how important Quantz and other local thinkers regarded simplicity and directness in music, as opposed to the *bizzarria* that Quantz criticized in Vivaldi's late works. However much he might have learned by studying the contrapuntal and harmonic complexities of his father's music, he would have understood that these, too, were not to be incorporated in large numbers into his own compositions.[13] Another element of the same aesthetic was the skepticism if not outright hostility toward Baroque word painting expressed by other contemporary writers. Friedrich Wilhelm Marpurg, reporting Christian Bach's presence at the premiere of Graun's oratorio *Tod Jesu* in March 1755, claimed that Christian was so moved by one passage that he "could not refrain from recognizing this expression of Graun's, simple as it is, as a pictorial master stroke" (see example 5.1).[14] Although Marpurg writes here of a musical "painting" (*Gemählde*), what probably excited J. C. Bach (or at least Marpurg) in this passage was not an old-fashioned symbolic representation of a word or image in the text. Rather it must have been the interruption of the simple homophonic texture that Graun uses for the first line of the aria—a typical example of "Berlin classicism"—by the suddenly energetic scale for the violins that follows. This reflects, without exactly "painting," the words "theilt die Wolken" (opens the clouds).

---

rather than at the end of the last solo episode; see, e.g., the first movement of the Concerto in F Minor (Warb C 73), composed before J. C. Bach departed from Berlin. Benda does much the same in the corresponding movement of his Violin Concerto in D Minor, Lee 2.4 (better known in a version in E Minor for flute, Lee 2.9).

13. In his *Versuch einer Anweisung die Flöte traversiere zu spielen* (Berlin, 1752), chap. 18, para. 58, Quantz criticizes Vivaldi's *Frechheit* (the word *bizarrerie* appears in the simultaneously published French edition, *Essai d'une méthode pour apprendre à jouer de la flute traversière*); this is rendered as "eccentricity" in the translation by Edward R. Reilly, *On Playing the Flute*, 2d ed. (New York: Schirmer Books, 1985). Although praising Sebastian Bach as an organist (chap. 18, para. 83), Quantz withholds any commentary on his compositions, although this could be because these simply were not known widely enough to be worth commenting on. Later writers contrasted Sebastian negatively against Handel; see Schulenberg, *Music of C. P. E. Bach*, 267–68.

14. "Wenigstens konte der davon gerührte Londoner Bach . . . bey der sehr feinen Empfindung die her hatte, sich nicht enthalten, diesen Ausdruck des Grauns, so simpel er ist, für einen malerischen Meisterzug zu erkennen"; Friedrich Wilhelm Marpurg, *Legende einiger Musikheiligen* (Cologne, 1786), 306, quoted by Hans-Joachim Schulze, "Wann begann die 'italienische Reise' der jüngsten Bach-Sohnes?" *BJ* 69 (1983): 119–22 (on 121), trans. Stephanie Wollny as "When Did the Youngest Bach Son Begin His 'Italian Journey'?" in *J. C. Bach*, ed. Corneilson, 53. Schulze subsequently expressed some skepticism about Marpurg's memory of this incident in "Noch einmal: Wann begann die 'italienische Reise' der jüngsten Bach-Sohnes?" *BJ* 74 (1988): 235–36; reprinted in *J. C. Bach*, ed. Corneilson, 54.

Example 5.1. Carl Heinrich Graun, *Der Tod Jesu*, aria "Ein Gebeth um neue Stärke" (without bassoon doublings): (a) mm. 25–36; (b) mm. 41–44.

Although Graun avoids serious counterpoint, also notable here is his flexible use of compositional texture, which extends to the violins' heterophonic accompaniment of the following vocal phrase. But Bach (or Marpurg) was particularly struck by the composer's "simplicity"—perhaps meaning a certain directness of expression—in place of the more complex type of texture favored by the generation of Georg Philipp Telemann and Sebastian Bach. The new approach was typical of Graun, who acknowledged avoiding the sharp dissonances and other complications of the older style, which tended to focus the musical expression on individual words.[15] In the same vein, Emanuel Bach would describe his Gellert-Lieder of a few years later as being composed with an eye toward "the whole song."[16] To be sure, the composer of a strophic song or lied had to view the entire text as a whole, but Emanuel would also remain closer to Graun than to his own father in his approach to arias and choruses—and the same was even more true of Christian. Baroque-style word painting is largely absent from his vocal music, as it is from Mozart's. Yet Mozart and even J. C. Bach would resist the aesthetic of simplicity, and neither was afraid to employ harsh dissonances or sudden contrasts when a text or a dramatic situation called for it. The variability of both musical texture and emotional affect in the passage from *Tod Jesu* would also be a fundamental element in the music of both.

Why Christian Bach left Berlin by mid-1755 is unknown. Perhaps he had been given to understand that no position in the royal chamber music would be forthcoming; that went instead to Carl Fasch, son of the composer Johann Friedrich Fasch and also a pupil of Emanuel. Once in Italy, Christian followed the precedent established by another member of a German organist dynasty who went south, converting to Catholicism and becoming a popular composer in all the current Italian vocal and instrumental genres. Like Hasse, whom he might have met during the latter's visit to Berlin in 1753, Christian would eventually marry an Italian singer—although his mother was also a professional vocalist. Indeed, J. C. Bach had grown up in a household in which up-to-date Italian vocal music, including works like Giovanni Battista Pergolesi's *Stabat mater*, was cultivated alongside more old-fashioned Latin polyphony.[17]

15. Graun described his approach to text-setting in a letter of 9 November 1751 to Telemann, no. 98 in Georg Philipp Telemann, *Briefwechsel*, ed. Hans Grosse and Hans Rudolf Jung (Leipzig: Deutscher Verlag für Musik, 1972), 279; see also Peter John Czornyj, "Georg Philipp Telemann (1681–1767): His Relationship to Carl Heinrich Graun and the Berlin Circle" (PhD. diss, University of Hull, 1988), 237.

16. "Das ganze Lied"; preface (*Vorrede*) to *Herrn Professor Gellerts Geistliche Oden und Lieder mit Melodien* (Berlin, 1758), Wq 194; ed. and trans. Darrell M. Berg in CPEB:CW, VI/1, xviii.

17. J. S. Bach performed the Pergolesi work in a version with the German parody text *Tilge, Höchster, meine Sünden* (BWV 1083); a figured organ part (in D-B, Mus. ms. 17155/16) copied jointly by J. S. Bach and his future son-in-law J. C. Altnickol is dated c. 1746–47, indicating a performance in Leipzig when J. C. Bach was about twelve years old.

Exploration of both idioms might therefore be considered part of a "Bach tradition." Latin polyphony was not ignored at Berlin, as Emanuel demonstrated with several movements in his Magnificat of 1749,[18] but none of the other Bach sons and pupils took it up nearly as enthusiastically as Christian did after his arrival in Italy. There he studied counterpoint with Padre Martini, submitting for the latter's approval some of the Latin church music in which he cultivated imitative polyphony far more assiduously than his older brothers did.[19]

Today this music, like Christian's operas, is only just becoming known. Evaluating it has been made difficult by the absence of a genuine critical edition, but, as recordings of the composer's major vocal works have gradually been made available, it has become clear that his style is distinct from that of Italianate works by other composers of the 1750s. For instance, his scoring tends to be richer, involving not only inventive use of woodwind instruments but relatively elaborate accompaniment textures. These anticipate the type of contrapuntal accompaniment that would become characteristic of Mozart's mature music. Chromaticism anticipating Mozart is also common—both the decorative type that involves local inflections and the more substantial type that involves lasting modulations.

How this style emerged with apparent suddenness in Christian Bach's Italian compositions of the 1750s has yet to be established. Of his contemporaries, his older friend and performing colleague Carl Friedrich Abel perhaps came closest to following a similar stylistic evolution. Abel apparently began composing in the idiom favored at Dresden and Berlin, as in the seemingly early op. 6 flute sonatas.[20] By the time he established himself at London (in 1758 or 1759), he must already have been writing in the early Classical style characteristic of his better-known works, among them the symphony copied out by Mozart and misattributed to the latter as K 18 (Anh. 51). Abel, however, seems never to have composed any substantial vocal music, and although he may even have briefly studied with J. S. Bach, he lacked the youngest Bach son's immersion in both the Bach tradition and the Italian contrapuntal tradition.

To be sure, Christian Bach was not ashamed to write large quantities of innocuous instrumental music, in an idiom that has given him the modern reputation of being a

18. Whether the Magnificat, composed in 1749 at Berlin, was also performed there is unknown; see Christine Blanken's introduction to CPEB:CW, V/1.1, xvi.

19. Stephen Roe first drew attention to J. C. Bach's correspondence with Martini in "J. C. Bach, 1735–1782: Towards a New Biography," *Musical Times* 123 (1982): 23–26, mentioning in particular that "Bach studied strict counterpoint with Martini in Bologna and submitted his church compositions, written in Milan, for his teacher's advice and correction."

20. Although published only in 1763 at London, these fall into the slow-fast-moderate sequence of movements favored at Berlin, and in other respects they also recall the style of Quantz and especially Graun.

Example 5.2. J. C. Bach, Sonata in F Major (Warb B 20), mvt. 1, mm. 1–6.

pale precursor of the adult Mozart. Support for this view could be found in numerous pieces first composed probably in Italy during the 1750s (see, e.g., his Sonata in F Major, Warb B 20 in example 5.2). Like Telemann—who also remains best known for the least important part of his large output—Christian Bach would later publish dozens of sonatas and other pieces for various combinations of keyboard, strings, and winds, in a popular, unchallenging style that appealed to amateurs. He seems also to have been more comfortable than his brothers in repeating *galant* formulas, including many of those so-called schemata or tropes codified by Robert Gjerdingen.[21]

Even during his Italian period, J. C. Bach was capable of writing much more distinctive music; works composed after his arrival in England, in 1762, include many further instances. One relatively familiar example is the Symphony in E-flat Major (Warb C 26) for double orchestra, possibly written in 1772, whose initial theme, introduced in unison, is subsequently developed contrapuntally (example 5.3). Already in his first major datable composition, the *Messa de' morti* composed in 1757 at Milan, J. C. Bach included a *Dies irae* (Warb E 12) whose bold strokes probably go beyond anything in his subsequent Italian compositions (example 5.4). Yet music of equal audacity occurs in his lone French opera, *Amadis des Gaules*, performed at Paris in 1779 and subsequently issued in a posthumous printed edition. Particularly notable is the scene in which the sorceress Arcabonne raises the spirit of her dead brother Ardan (example 5.5).

21. Robert Gjerdingen, *Music in the Galant Style* (New York: Oxford University Press, 2007).

Example 5.3. J. C. Bach, Symphony in E-flat Major, Forster op. 18, no. 1
(Warb C 26), mvt. 1, mm. 1–9 (without winds).

Example 5.4. J. C. Bach, *Messa de' morti*, *Dies irae* (Warb E 12),
"Quantus tremor," mm. 11–17.

Example 5.5. J. C. Bach, *Amadis des Gaules* (Warb G 39), excerpt from act 2, scene 2.

Whether Mozart knew *Amadis* or the earlier *Dies irae* is uncertain, but both works reveal a serious undercurrent in J. C. Bach's music that we might tentatively associate with the family tradition.[22] Still, dramatic writing like that of J. C. Bach's *Dies irae* could also be found in works by Hasse and others. Incantation scenes had a long tradition going back to Jean-Baptiste Lully, as Geoffrey Burgess has pointed out.[23] The young Mozart might have modeled some of his first published works, notably the accompanied sonatas (K 6–9) published at Paris in 1764, on similar publications such as Christian's op. 2 (c. 1763). Others, however, including Abel, were publishing similar things, and in any case the style of J. C. Bach's simpler instrumental publications is probably too generic to have furnished a unique, identifiable model. Even if J. C. Bach served as a personal role model for Mozart, clearer evidence is needed to demonstrate his channeling of a family tradition to the younger musician.

Counterpoint

The simple counterpoint of J. C. Bach's symphony (Warb C 26) is remote from anything by Sebastian. Mozart could have adopted the underlying idea directly from Christian Bach. Both composers left multiple instances of unison opening themes that are later developed contrapuntally (examples 5.6 and 5.7). Yet the basic idea could be traced to any fugal composition, including Sebastian's inventions, which Christian probably studied as a child. Something closer to the later Classical procedure occurs in Emanuel Bach's First Württemberg Sonata, Wq 49/1, where a portion of the opening theme is later copied to the bass (example 5.8).

Even this limited use of counterpoint is unusual for Emanuel Bach. Christian, however, would be the one Bach son to take up counterpoint wholeheartedly, in the Latin church music composed in Italy. Among the examples is the Kyrie from his Mass for the Dead, one of the works that Christian submitted to Padre Martini (example 5.9)—who seems to have replaced his actual father (and his half-brother) as a mentor. Christian's exercises in this vein recall the music in the *stile antico*—both his own and that of others—which Sebastian Bach had been cultivating especially during the 1740s, when Christian was growing up in Leipzig. These included the final additions to the

---

22. That Mozart may have heard the *Dies irae* during a visit to Milan in 1770 is argued by Murl Sickbert, "The Mozarts in Milan, February 9–10, 1770: A Funeral Performance of Johann Christian Bach's *Dies irae* and Vespers Music?" *Mozart-Jahrbuch* (1991): 461–67. Mozart was in Paris in 1778, when J. C. Bach was making preparations for *Amadis*, but it is unlikely that any of the music had yet been composed, and it is unknown whether Mozart later saw its posthumously published score.

23. Geoffrey Burgess, "Enlightening Harmonies: Rameau's *corps sonore* and the Representation of the Divine in the *tragédie en musique*," *JAMS* 65 (2012): 383–462, esp. 387–91. Burgess refers to these scenes as "oracular."

Example 5.6. J. C. Bach, Duetto in F Major, Welcker op. 18, no. 6 (Warb A 20), mvt. 1:
(a) mm. 1–4, (b) mm. 56–59.

Example 5.7. W. A. Mozart, Sonata in D Major, κ 576, mvt. 1: (a) mm. 1–5, (b) mm.
9–10, (c) mm. 28–30.

Example 5.8. (a) J. S. Bach, Invention no. 11 in G minor, BWV 782, mm. 1–4; (b) C. P. E. Bach, "Württemberg Sonata" no. 1 in A Minor, Wq 49/1, mm. 1–2 and 9b-11a.

Mass in B Minor—the opening movement of the Credo and the "Confiteor"—as well as the *Art of Fugue*. Unlike Sebastian's exercises in *stile antico*, however, Christian's seem generic, like so much Italianate counterpoint of the period. Thus, they avoid harsh dissonances, unusual melodic intervals, and other distinctive features now associated not only with J. S. Bach but with the expressive *stile moderno* of the Baroque generally. But there is little reason to connect them to Mozart, whose music shows few signs of his following J. C. Bach's cultivation of this brand of counterpoint.

A more individual example of counterpoint is the fugue in Christian's Sonata in C Minor, op. 5, no. 6, possibly drafted in Italy but published only in 1766 after the composer came to London (example 5.10). This fugue, too, has little to do with any examples by Sebastian, nor those composed by Emanuel in the years after their fa-

Example 5.9. J. C. Bach, *Messa de' morti*, Kyrie (Warb E 11), mm. 1–9
(without instrumental doublings).

ther's death.[24] On the other hand, Stephen Roe has compared this sonata with the examples published twenty-four years earlier by Padre Martini.[25] The fugues in those sonatas are in current Italian style (not *stile antico*), and Martini's procedure of opening each sonata with a prelude and fugue must have served as a precedent for Christian's doing the same. Christian treats his fugue subject in a more Classical way, however, splitting off the first three notes as a motive for development in the episodes—the same sort of treatment given to unison themes in some of his symphonies and other works (compare examples 5.6 and 5.10b). On the other hand, this movement is, like Christian's Kyrie, a double fugue that introduces its two subjects at the outset (as Roe

24. None of Emanuel's keyboard fugues, nor those of Friedemann Bach, is part of a larger multimovement work, unless one counts Emanuel's Fantasia and Fugue, Wq 119/7, and several fugues contained within Friedemann's multisectional fantasias.

25. Stephen Roe, "The Keyboard Sonatas of Johann Christian Bach (1735–1782)," in *The Early Keyboard Sonata in Italy and Beyond*, ed. Rohan H. Stewart-MacDonald (Turnhout, Belg.: Brepols, 2016), 191–207, esp. 197.

Example 5.10. J. C. Bach, Sonata in C Minor, op. 5, no. 6 (Warb A 6),
mvt. 2, (a) mm. 1–5, (b) mm. 62–65.

observed). The device was common in Italian fugues of the time, including those in
Martini's sonatas, but it was rarely used by J. S. Bach.

Mozart surely knew this piece, the last of Christian's op. 5 sonatas, although it was
not one of the three pieces from the set that the young Mozart turned into concertos.[26]
The presence of fugue would have made its conversion into a concerto a very different
exercise from his arrangement of any of the other sonatas of op. 5, in which orchestration and the manipulation of sonata form were the chief concerns, not counterpoint.
One of the complications that Leopold Mozart would regret in his son's later music
was surely his fascination with imitative and chromatic counterpoint. By then, although
the music of J. S. Bach might already have been gaining recognition from some con-
noisseurs, it had also become a cliché to view his archaic polyphony as being of purely
technical interest, as opposed to the genuinely expressive music of George Frideric
Handel. The younger Mozart might even have shared this view to some degree; after
all, he performed at least two major vocal works of Handel but none by J. S. Bach.[27]

26. Nevertheless, there is, surprisingly, a clear echo of the passage shown in example 5.10b in the
Rondo alla turca from Mozart's Sonata K 331, mm. 9–16.

27. During his 1764 visit to London as a child, Mozart played solos in the intermissions of Handel's
Acis and Galatea; he later performed the work itself, as well as *Messiah*, with his own expanded orchestration in 1788 and 1789, respectively.

Example 5.11. (a) W. A. Mozart, Prelude (Fantasia) and Fugue in C Minor, к 394,
fugue, mm. 1–5; (b) Suite in C Major, к 399, mvt. 1, mm. 68–74.

The closest the mature Mozart came to directly imitating Sebastian's counterpoint
might have been in the deliberately cerebral fugues of K 394, 399, and 426 (examples
5.11 and 5.12). Each indulges a perverse pleasure in dissonant counterpoint, combined
in K 426 with sometimes *récherché* modulations. Clearly inspired by J. S. Bach—the
chromatic appoggiaturas in the subject of K 426 echo the fugue in B Minor from the
first book of the *Well-Tempered Clavier*, and they incorporate the B-A-C-H motive
(formed from the letters of Bach's name) in retrograde—each fugue is just as clearly
unlike anything composed by Sebastian. Moreover, the fugue subject of K 426, with
its canonic treatment, might actually be traced to a symphony by Franz Joseph Haydn,
although there is no evidence that Mozart knew that work (example 5.13).

Example 5.12. W. A. Mozart, Fugue in C Minor, K 426: (a) mm. 10–14, (b) mm. 44–48.

An earlier work, the Fugue in G Minor, K 401, might have had a similar inspiration, although it is less "Bachisch" in its mildly dissonant and conventionally chromatic counterpoint than in its design: It presents first the *rectus*, then the *inversus* forms of the subject before combining them, as do several fugues from the *Well-Tempered Clavier*, although K 401 lacks the stretto expositions that Bach also tends to include when demonstrating the contrapuntal potential of a fugue subject. The relatively

Example 5.13. F. J. Haydn, Symphony in D Minor, "Lamentatione,"
Hob I:26, mvt. 3, mm. 32–36.

early date of K 401—now thought to have preceded the other fugues mentioned above—might raise doubts that Mozart was inspired to write it by acquaintance with the music of J. S. Bach.[28] Yet Padre Martini, whom Mozart had visited in 1770, was not unfamiliar with the elder Bach's contrapuntal works, owning printed exemplars of the *Musical Offering* and part 3 of the *Clavierübung*, as well as manuscript copies of selections from the *Well-Tempered Clavier*. Indeed, Martini might be considered alongside J. C. Bach as a potential transmitter of the Bach tradition to Mozart. But the latter would, in any case, have made his own selection of elements from Sebastian's fugues for further development—just as he incorporated other aspects of Baroque style into the fragmentary suite K 399. That any of those elements could be traced specifically to Mozart's contacts with J. C. Bach is unlikely, even if Mozart's mature contrapuntal compositions can be placed within the Bach tradition, considered broadly.

Symphonic Writing

As important as the counterpoint in examples 5.3, 5.6, and 5.7 is the spacious phrasing and the rigorous motivic work. Both would be important features of the mature Classical style, particularly in the emerging genre of the symphony. At a time when a symphony might still be little more than a noisy way of opening a concert or a night at the theater, Christian Bach's works of this type could have expanded Mozart's idea of what a symphony could be, in terms of length and seriousness. We might even

28. I am grateful to Robert Marshall for reminding me of this work, once thought to date from 1782 but placed a decade earlier by Wolfgang Plath, "Beiträge zur Mozart-Autographie II: Schriftchronologie 1770–1780," *Mozart-Jahrbuch* (1976–77): 131–73, see esp. 161.

construe the serious cultivation of the symphony as part of a Bach tradition, albeit not one going all the way back to Sebastian. For Christian had been preceded by his half-brothers Friedemann and Emanuel in composing symphonies that went somewhat beyond the traditional overture type of the mid-eighteenth century. Equally important are a number of keyboard sonatas and chamber compositions by Emanuel that adopt what can be called a "symphonic style."

Three of Emanuel's symphonies date from Christian Bach's last year at Berlin.[29] In these works, as in others of the period, Emanuel Bach was tending away from the dramatic, sometimes startling character of his best-known works of the 1740s, such as the Concerto in D Minor, Wq 23. Now he was composing music that can be surprisingly close to that which we identify with Christian Bach, as in a keyboard sonata that the latter must have copied out for his brother not long before he left for Italy (example 5.14). The symphonic style of the first movement of this sonata has echoes in Christian Bach's op. 5 sonatas and other keyboard compositions (including the four-hand sonata illustrated in example 5.6). Final movements in many of the same sonatas frequently follow the simple rondo form that Emanuel first used during the early 1750s.[30] But in what sense could such music be said to belong to a Bach tradition? Sebastian had taken up popular styles, making them his own in works such as the "Italian Concerto" and the homage cantatas for the Saxon court. Now, even as Emanuel was adopting the style of his colleagues at the Berlin court, the slow movement of this sonata incorporates the chromatic voice leading and written-out melodic embellishment that were Emanuel Bach's legacy from his father (example 5.15).

Neal Zaslaw heard a reflection of the "Hamburg" Bach in a harmonic surprise in the symphony K 19 of 1765.[31] Yet in 1765 Emanuel was still in Berlin, and whether Mozart knew any of his music at that point is impossible to say. In principle, however, Mozart might have learned of such things through Christian, who, as a boy, must have heard many sophisticated harmonic strokes in improvisations by his father as well as his older brother. From them he must also have gained an intuitive mastery and

---

29. These are Wq 174, 175, and 176 in C, F, and D Major, respectively. The chronological list of works in the composer's estate catalog gives the year (1755) and place of origin (Berlin or Potsdam) but does not indicate whether these were written before Christian's departure. See *Verzeichniß des musikalischen Nachlasses des verstorbenen Capellmeisters Carl Philipp Emanuel Bach* (Hamburg: Schniebes, 1790); transcription online at http://www.cpebach.org/pdfs/resources/NV-1790.pdf.

30. On Emanuel's "symphonic" keyboard sonatas and other instrumental compositions of the 1750s and later, see Schulenberg, *Music of C. P. E. Bach*, chaps. 7 and 9.

31. Neal Zaslaw, *Mozart's Symphonies: Context, Performance Practice, Reception* (Oxford: Oxford University Press, 1989), 47, referring to a sudden A-sharp at the start of the development in the first movement (m. 46). Something remarkably similar occurs at the corresponding point in J. C. Bach's Symphony in E-flat Major, op. 6, no. 5.

Example 5.14. C. P. E. Bach, Sonata in E-flat Major, Wq 65/28, mvt. 1, mm. 1–13.

Example 5.15. C. P. E. Bach, Sonata in E-flat Major, Wq 65/28, mvt. 2, mm. 1–4.

understanding of sophisticated harmony and voice leading at an early age—more so, one suspects, than Mozart, who must have grown up hearing relatively conventional music. But the rare harmonic surprises in his early works, like his use of symphonic style in general, can hardly be traced unequivocally to any Bach tradition. His earliest symphonies, even those presumably composed immediately after meeting J. C. Bach, are less obviously inspired by the latter than somewhat more mature ones. Echoes of Christian's music grow clearer around the time of K 81 of 1770, whose three movements all seem deliberately modeled on types found in J. C. Bach's op. 3 symphonies (1765). Much the same could be said of the concluding rondo of K 73, although that work is in four movements, unlike any symphony certainly composed by J. C. Bach. By 1772, Mozart could open the slow movement of K 129 with an almost simplisti-

Example 5.16. (a) W. A. Mozart, Symphony in G Major, к 129, mvt. 2, mm. 1–8;
(b) J. C. Bach, Concerto ("o Sinfonia") in D Major, op. 1, no. 6, mvt. 2, mm. 1–4.

cally symmetrical theme that is practically a caricature of the older composer (example 5.16). The development section of the same movement is a brief fugato, yet this too must reflect the still-young Mozart's assimilation of ideas taken specifically from J. C. Bach, not from an older Bach tradition.

Other Elements of Composition

Could there be other elements of Mozart's style traceable through J. C. Bach to some Bach family tradition? J. C. Bach was an innovator in the use of instrumental color and new orchestral textures; Ann van Allen-Russell has argued that his use of timbre was not simply decorative or ornamental but is a fundamental element of his music.[32]

32. Ann van Allen-Russell, "Wind Orchestration in the Music of Johann Christian Bach, 1762–1782: Studies in Structure, Texture and Form" (PhD diss., University of London, 2004), 148–86.

Claims of this sort are hard to substantiate objectively; we lack a ready vocabulary for analyzing timbre or sound comparable to that for harmony and form. But J. C. Bach's imaginative use of wind instruments has long been recognized,[33] and similar inventiveness extends to the variegated textures of his keyboard and chamber music. These features of his music could have been a legacy from his father, reflecting the careful scoring of the latter's vocal works, as well as his organ registrations that could unnerve organ makers when their instruments were tested.[34]

A striking manifestation of Christian's interest in orchestral color occurs in the incantation scene from *Amadis*, which employs a sort of *Klangfarbenmelodie* as a single diminished-seventh chord is sustained by three trombones, which are then joined by clarinets and eventually the entire woodwind section (see example 5.5 above). This example is exceptional; more typical is the use of brief passages for solo or massed woodwinds to provide varied orchestral color within a symphonic movement or aria, as in *Adriano in Siria* (example 5.17). Scoring such as this might have been among the prompts for Charles Burney's declaration that Christian Bach "seems to have been the first composer who observed the law of *contrast*, as a *principle*."[35] The remark follows a less positive evaluation of Christian's arias, which are praised less for their melodies than for "the richness of the accompaniments"; this could be read as a criticism of their contrapuntal character.

Mid-century Berlin had already seen Quantz insisting on *Mannigfaltigkeit* (variety), at least in performance; his pupil Christoph Nichelmann followed him, requiring the same *Mannigfaltigkeit* in "harmony."[36] To be sure, Nichelmann had also studied with Sebastian Bach, and a commitment to contrast or variety, whether of harmony, texture, or instrumental color, could be understood as an element of the Bach tradition. But the variety that Burney describes was one of expressive character; Christian Bach might have learned to use it as much from Graun (see example 5.1 above) as from older family members. In keyboard music, J. C. Bach was probably less likely than his contemporaries to rely on a single type of accompaniment throughout a given move-

---

33. See, e.g., Eric Weimer, *"Opera Seria" and the Evolution of Classical Style 1755–1772* (Ann Arbor, MI: UMI Research Press, 1984), esp. 112–13 on woodwind scoring by J. C. Bach, as compared to that of Hasse and Niccolò Jommelli.

34. As Emanuel Bach reported to Johann Nicolaus Forkel in a letter of (probably) 1774, in NBR, 396; 3:284–85, no. 801.

35. Charles Burney, *A General History of Music*, 4 vols. (London, 1776–89), 4:483. This frequently quoted comment referred in the first instance to alternations between loud and quiet passages in Christian's orchestral music, which, according to Burney, "seldom failed, after a rapid and noisy passage to introduce one that was slow and soothing."

36. Quantz, *Versuch*, chap. 11, para. 3, and chap. 14, para. 25; Christoph Nichelmann, *Die Melodie nach ihrem Wesen* (Danzig, 1755), esp. chaps. 36 and 41.

Example 5.17. J. C. Bach, *Adriano in Siria* (Warb G 6), aria
"Deh, lascia, o ciel pietoso," mm. 31–49.

Example 5.18. J. C. Bach, Sonata in E Major, op. 5, no. 5 (Warb A 5), mvt. 1, mm. 26–31.

Example 5.19. W. A. Mozart, Sonata in B-flat Major, K. 10, mvt. 1, mm. 13–18.

ment, rather varying the texture every few measures (example 5.18). Mozart, even as a child, could likewise flit rapidly from one texture to another, as in passages from his early accompanied sonatas (example 5.19). This, like Mozart's writing for winds, could have been something learned from J. C. Bach, but, again, it is difficult to see it as part of a specific Bach tradition.

Conclusions

It is beginning to look as if the answers to the questions posed at the beginning of this exploration must be largely negative. Such a conclusion should not be surprising, given the restless originality of both J. C. Bach and Mozart. Even on those occasions when each quoted from his predecessors, the citations, although presumably intended as homage, also illustrate how far each had come from his models. One of Christian's Magnificats (Warb E 22) opens with an apparent quotation from Emanuel's setting of the same text (note also the similar brass writing in examples 5.20 and 5.21). Yet it continues as a typically concise Catholic setting, sharply distinct from the more extended Lutheran Magnificats of both Sebastian and Emanuel. J. C. Bach's accompanied sonata, op. 10, no. 1, opens by quoting Sebastian's Partita no. 1, BWV 825, then repeats Sebastian's theme in simple imitation (examples 5.22 and 5.23). But the movement unfolds in a manner typical for Christian, constituting a "type 2" sonata-form movement.[37] Both works, while perhaps paying tribute to his father and his brother, also declare J. C. Bach's independence from them. The resulting compositions are simpler than theirs, in the absence of complex counterpoint and harmony, but they are arguably richer in their instrumentation and variety of texture.

Mozart's appropriation of a theme by Christian for the slow movement of K 414 is of a like nature: the borrowed first four measures are followed by a new phrase that is distinctly his own, recognizable as such by its chromatic cadential formula (example 5.24).[38] Mozart's earlier adaptations of three of J. C. Bach's keyboard sonatas as concertos are of less interest in the present context, as they leave the original compositions essentially intact, merely adding orchestral frames (ritornellos) and interludes for each movement. Of greater relevance are Mozart's settings of the aria text "Non so d'onde viene" from Christian Bach's *Alessandro nell'Indie*.[39] Resetting the poetry of Pietro

37. The terminology is that of James A. Hepokoski and Warren Darcy, *Elements of Sonata Theory: Norms, Types, and Deformations of the Late Eighteenth-Century Sonata* (New York: Oxford University Press, 2006). A "type 2" movement is essentially a sonata-allegro that lacks a so-called double return to mark the beginning of a distinct recapitulation section, although the authors rightly reject this formulation as ahistoric (see esp. chap. 17).

38. There seems to be no basis for a suggestion that the continuation of the phrase might be "perhaps by someone else," as proposed by Ellwood Derr, "Some Thoughts on the Design of Mozart's Opus 4, the 'Subscription Concertos' (K. 414, 413, and 415)," in *Mozart's Piano Concertos: Text, Context, Interpretation*, ed. Neal Zaslaw (Ann Arbor: University of Michigan Press, 1996), 187–210, esp. 205. Whether the same three concertos contain further quotations from J. C. Bach, as Derr argues, depends on whether the highly approximate parallels constitute what Charles Rosen described as "standard formulas, without much idiosyncratic character, that . . . would appear in the work of any late eighteenth-century composer," in his review of the same publication, in *JAMS* 51 (1998): 373–84 (quotation on 374).

39. The aria text is actually from Pietro Metastasio's *L'Olimpiade*; in J. C. Bach's *Alessandro* the aria replaces the title character's "Serbati a grandi imprese," as part of a shortened version of the opening of act 3.

Example 5.20. J. C. Bach, Magnificat (Warb E 22), opening chorus,
mm. 15–18 (without viola doubling bass).

Example 5.21. C. P. E. Bach, Magnificat, Wq 215, opening chorus,
mm. 22–25 (without oboe and viola doublings).

Example 5.22. J. C. Bach, Sonata in B-flat Major, Welcker op. 10, no. 1 (Warb B 2), mvt. 1, mm. 5–11.

Example 5.23. J. S. Bach, Partita no. 1 in B-flat Major, BWV 825, mvt. 1, mm. 1–3.

Metastasio was, of course, a standard practice for eighteenth-century composers. But Christian was not the only member of the Bach family with whom Mozart shared texts; the song "Im Frühlingsgesang," K 597, has a lyric by Christian Fürchtegott Gellert that was previously set by C. P. E. Bach, in a publication that Mozart could have known.[40]

What stands out in each of Mozart's settings of these two poems is how different they are from those of his predecessors.[41] In Peter Williams's phrase, they deliberately

40. The two settings are compared in Schulenberg, *Music of C. P. E. Bach*, 178.

41. This is true even if the two Metastasio settings share significant features with one another and even with earlier settings of the same text by Pergolesi; see Stefan Kunze, "Die Vertonungen der Aria 'Non so d'onde viene' von J. Chr. Bach und Mozart," *Analecta Musicologica* 2 (1965): 85–110, esp. 109–10; reprinted in *J. C. Bach*, ed. Corneilson, 435–62.

Example 5.24. (a) W. A. Mozart, Piano Concerto in A Major, K 414, mvt. 2, mm. 1–8 (without figured solo part); (b) J. C. Bach, overture to *La calamita dei cuori* (Warb G 27), mvt. 2, mm. 1–4.

"swerve away" from music that could have inspired them or provided a compositional model. The underlying concept was implicit in Johann Nicolaus Forkel's famous observation that the older Bach sons intentionally avoided imitating their father "because they could never have equaled him in his style."[42] The idea is *explicit* in Mozart's letter of 28 February 1778 to his father, in which he mentions his intention to make his first setting of the aria text "Non so d'onde viene" "totally unlike" J. C. Bach's setting (example 5.25a-b).[43] When Mozart returned to Metastasio's poem in 1787, he apparently decided to swerve away from his own younger self as well (example 25c). His second setting begins seriously enough, but its quicker B section has almost a buffa character.

42. Johann Nicolaus Forkel, *Ueber Johann Sebastian Bachs Leben, Kunst und Kunstwerke* (Leipzig, 1802), 44; NBR, 458.

43. LMF, 497; MBA, 2:304.

Example 5.25. Opening vocal line (all without winds) from (a) J. C. Bach, aria "Non so d'onde viene," from *Alessandro nell' Indie* (Warb G 3); (b) W. A. Mozart, aria "Non so d'onde viene," k 294; (c), W. A. Mozart, aria "Non so d'onde viene," k 512.

Both settings, however, give the orchestra a more varied and busier accompaniment than J. C. Bach's.

Mozart was not the only composer of the later eighteenth century to make his music more complicated than his models. In this he might even have followed J. C. Bach, for, as Burney's comments suggest, both resisted the prevailing aesthetic of simplicity. It is therefore ironic that Leopold Mozart would hold up J. C. Bach to his son as a model composer of simple, accessible music, praising what he called Bach's *Kleinigkeiten* or "trifles" and urging his son to write something equally "short, easy and popular."[44] From the context, Leopold appears to have been urging his son to write something like Christian Bach's op. 8 flute quartets, which had come out six years earlier, in 1772. Leopold Mozart's thoughts about simplicity might well have been influenced, or at least ratified, by what he had read in Quantz's book, which Christian Bach also must have known.[45] In fact, Christian's flute quartets are not particularly simple, at least from the point of view of texture, as when Bach writes an Alberti-type accompaniment for the violin and simultaneously a countermelody for the viola (example 5.26). On the other hand, this piece comprises only two movements, and the second is an almost perfunctory little minuet.

After the accompanied keyboard sonatas of his childhood, Mozart never published anything so simple. In his avoidance of the "short, easy, and popular" Mozart followed his own inclinations, as he also did when he found inspiration in the music of J. S. Bach. Even if he had been encouraged to do so by Christian Bach himself, the unavoidable conclusion is that the hypothesis of a Bach tradition passed down to Mozart through J. C. Bach cannot be sustained. There is, nevertheless, a peculiar coincidence that unites J. S. Bach, J. C. Bach, and Mozart: each died leaving behind a major work that was in some sense unfinished. Sebastian's *Art of Fugue* and Mozart's Requiem are well known; J. C. Bach's opera *Amadis* is not. Stephen Roe, however, has traced the successful effort by Christian Bach's widow, the singer Cecilia Grassi, to see his last and greatest opera published posthumously.[46] As Roe demonstrates, the printed score was intended to reflect the composer's intentions more closely than did its badly cut first performance.

---

44. Letter of 13 August 1778 in LMF, 599; MBA, 2:444.

45. Leopold listed Quantz among the authors on which he drew for the short history of music that prefaces his *Versuch einer gründlichen Violinschule* (Augsburg, 1756), 17.

46. Stephen Roe, "Johann Christian Bach and Cecilia Grassi: The Publication of 'Amadis de Gaule,'" in *The Sons of Bach: Essays for Elias N. Kulukundis*, ed. Peter Wollny and Stephen Roe (Ann Arbor, MI: Steglein, 2016), 158–73. Roe dates the publication of *Amadis* to "c. 1783–1784" as "most likely" (164). See also Roe, "Johann Christian Bach and Cecilia Grassi: Portrait of a Marriage," in *The Sons of Bach*, 134–57.

Example 5.26. J. C. Bach, Quartet in C Major, Welcker op. 8,
no. 1 (Warb B 51), mvt. 1, mm. 11–14.

Mozart's Requiem was not, of course, intended for publication. Yet it is, like both the *Art of Fugue* and *Amadis*, an encyclopedic masterpiece, demonstrating its composer's accomplishment in various types of music. It was merely a coincidence that work on these compositions, or their publication, was cut short by death. But the stories of all three works make clear to what degree the three composers shared a concern for consummate compositional craft. This, like the concern for swerving away from their predecessors, was not unique to the Bach tradition, but it was an essential part of it.

Doles and the Prefect of the Choir

New Observations on Mozart's Visit to the Thomasschule

Michael Maul

Among all the memorable reactions to J. S. Bach, Wolfgang Amadeus Mozart's visit to the Thomasschule in Leipzig in the spring of 1789 ranks among the most famous ones. Despite the fact that Mozart himself had earlier come across Bach's compositions and developed a certain enthusiasm for his keyboard music, his unexpected encounter with Bach's vocal music at the Thomasschule yielded his most famous expression concerning the role of Bach and the quality of the Thomaner.

However, unfortunately, no documents by Mozart himself about this memorable event have survived.[1] All the information concerning his stay in Leipzig is based on reports given later by eyewitnesses or people claiming to quote eyewitnesses, including figures such Johann Friedrich Rochlitz and Johann Friedrich Reichardt.

According to these materials, Mozart visited Leipzig twice—first on his way from Dresden to Berlin for some days after 20 April, and second after 12 May on his way back from Berlin.[2] It was during his first stay that he got the chance to visit the Thomasschule. (See figure 6.1.) The earliest report on this event was provided by Rochlitz

---

1. Only one of Mozart's letters from Leipzig has survived, dated 16 May 1789 in LMF, 925–26; MBA, 4:86–87. In this letter to Constanze, Wolfgang claims to have sent letters to her on 22 April from Leipzig, on 28 April and 5 May from Potsdam, and on 9 May from Leipzig. On 12 May 1789 Mozart gave a benefit concert at the Gewandhaus in Leipzig with the soprano Josepha Duschek. The concert program is listed in MDL, 300; MDB, 342.

2. On Mozart's journey to Dresden, Leipzig, and Berlin in general and his activities in Leipzig beyond his visit at the Thomasschule see Christoph Wolff, *Mozart at the Gateway to His Fortune: Serving the Emperor, 1788–1791* (New York: W. W. Norton, 2012), 50–71.

Figure 6.1. Engraving of the Thomaskirche and Thomasschule by
Balthasar Friedrich Leizelt. Courtesy of Michael Maul.

in the first volume of the *Allgemeine musikalische Zeitung*, published in November 1798
as part of a series of more or less reliable Mozart anecdotes.

> At the instigation of the late [Johann Friedrich] Doles, then cantor of the Leipzig
> Thomasschule, the choir surprised Mozart with the performance of the double-choir
> motet "Singet dem Herrn ein neues Lied"—a piece composed by the father of Ger-
> man music, Sebastian Bach. Mozart knew this Albrecht Dürer of German music more
> from hearsay than from his rarely performed compositions. As soon as the choir had
> sung a few bars, Mozart, fully astonished, looked up. A few bars later he exclaimed:
> "What is this!" And now, his entire soul seemed to be in his ears. At the end of the
> performance, Mozart shouted with joy: "That is definitely something from which
> one can learn a lot!" He was told that this school, where Sebastian Bach had served
> as cantor, owned the complete collection of Bach's motets and protected them like

a relic. "That is right, that is good," [Mozart] cried. "Show them to me." But there were no scores of these pieces; he therefore had them give him the manuscript parts. And now, it was pure joy for the silent observer to see how eagerly Mozart sat down, distributed the parts around himself, in both hands, on his knees, and on the chairs next to him, and, forgetting everything else, did not get up until he had gone through everything that was available by Sebastian Bach. He asked for a copy, held it in high esteem, and—if I am not mistaken—a real connoisseur of Bach's music and Mozart's Requiem . . . (especially of the great "Christe eleison" fugue) cannot fail to recognize how Mozart's mind studied, appreciated, and fully understood the spirit of the old contrapuntist's music.[3]

Rochlitz published other Mozart anecdotes, some of them focusing on his legendary generosity. Among them there is a short story that also refers to Mozart's visit to the Thomasschule.

When [Mozart] was visiting the Leipzig Thomasschule, and the choir sang some eight-voice motets in his honor, he confessed: "We don't have such a choir in Vienna, nor in Berlin and Prague." Among the crowd of at least forty singers he was particularly impressed by a certain bass singer. He started a short conversation with him and, without any of us present noticing anything, he pressed a handsome present into the young man's hand.[4]

3. *Allgemeine musikalische Zeitung* 1 (21 November 1798): 116–17: "Auf Veranstaltung des damaligen Kantors an der Thomasschule in Leipzig, des verstorbenen Doles, überraschte Mozarten das Chor mit der Aufführung der zweychörigen Motette; Singet dem Herrn ein neues Lied—von dem Altvater deutscher Musik, von Sebastian Bach. Mozart kannte diesen Albrecht Dürer der deutschen Musik mehr vom Hörensagen, als aus seinen selten gewordenen Werken. Kaum hatte das Chor einige Takte gesungen, so stuzte Mozart—noch einige Takte, da rief er: Was ist das?—und nun schien seine ganze Seele in seinen Ohren zu seyn. Als der Gesang geendigt war, rief er voll Freude: Das ist doch einmal etwas, woraus sich was lernen lässt!—Man erzählte ihm, dass diese Schule, an der Sebastian Bach Kantor gewesen war, die vollständige Sammlung seiner Motetten besitze und als eine Art Reliquien aufbewahre. Das ist recht, das ist brav—rief er; zeigen Sie her!—Man hatte aber keine Partitur dieser Gesänge; er liess sich also die ausgeschriebenen Stimmen geben—und nun war es für den stillen Beobachter eine Freude zu sehen, wie eifrig sich Mozart setzte, die Stimmen um sich herum, in beide Hände, auf die Kniee, auf die nächsten Stühle vertheilte, und, alles andere vergessend, nicht eher aufstand, bis er alles, was von Sebastian Bach da war, durchgesehen hatte. Er erbat sich eine Kopie, hielt diese sehr hoch, und—wenn ich nicht sehr irre, kann dem Kenner der Bachschen Kompositionen und des Mozartschen Requiem [. . .] besonders etwa der grossen Fuge Christe eleison—das Studium, die Werthschätzung, und die volle Auffassung des Geistes jenes alten Kontrapunktisten bey Mozarts zu allem fähigen Geiste, nicht entgehen." For further background on these anecdotes, see Maynard Solomon, "The Rochlitz Anecdotes: Issues of Authenticity in Early Mozart Biography," in *Mozart Studies*, ed. Cliff Eisen (Oxford: Clarendon Press, 1991), 1–59 (esp. 28).

4. *Allgemeine musikalische Zeitung* 6 (7 November 1798): 81: "Als er sich auf der Leipziger Thomasschule umsahe, und das Chor ihm zu Ehren einige achtstimmige Motetten sang, gestand er: So ein Chor haben wir in Wien nicht und hat man in Berlin und Prag nicht.—Unter der Menge von

Hans-Joachim Schulze has shown that both texts by Rochlitz, although sounding like fanciful legends with only a small amount of truth, are partly confirmed by other sources.[5] The most important is a report written by the philosopher Christian Friedrich Michaelis, published in the first volume of Johann Friedrich Reichardt's *Berlinische musikalische Zeitung* in 1805. His article also provides more specific information concerning the circumstances of Mozart's encounter with the choir. Michaelis, who in 1789 was a freshman at Leipzig University, remembered:

> On 22 April, without prior announcement, he [Mozart] played for free at the organ in the Thomaskirche. He played there for a full hour beautifully and artistically in front of numerous listeners. The then organist Görner and the late Cantor Doles were next to him, and pulled the stops. I saw him [Mozart] myself, a young and fashionably dressed young man, of medium height. Doles was completely delighted by the artist's playing and considered him the reincarnation of the old Sebastian Bach (his former teacher), for whom Mozart also expressed his heartfelt admiration, when listening to one of [Bach's] motets at the Thomasschule and studying his compositions there. Mozart had displayed all the harmonic arts with the greatest taste and ease, and improvised on themes, including the chorale "Jesu, meine Zuversicht," in the most glorious manner.[6]

In trying to determine whether Rochlitz's and Michaelis's reports on Mozart's visit to the Thomasschule were reliable, I came across some interesting new materials. The first concerns the encounter and its context: Mozart's visit took place at a very difficult time for Cantor Doles and the Thomasschule. After a long-lasting conflict between the Thomaskantor Johann Friedrich Doles and the Leipzig authorities, and a conspiracy between the Lord Mayor Carl Wilhelm Müller and his old friend Johann Adam Hiller (who planned his comeback in Leipzig in a leading musical position), Doles submitted his letter of resignation on 2 March 1789. He was the first Thomaskantor in history

---

wenigstens vierzig Sängern bemerkte er doch besonders einen Bassisten, der ihm sehr wohl gefiel. Er liess sich mit ihm in ein kleines Gespräch ein und ohne dass Einer von uns Anwesenden etwas bemerken konnte, drückte er dem jungen Mann ein für diesen ansehnliches Geschenk in die Hand." See also Soloman, "Rochlitz Anecdotes," 17–19.

5. Hans-Joachim Schulze, "'So ein Chor haben wir in Wien nicht'—Mozarts Begegnung mit dem Leipziger Thomanerchor und den Motetten Johann Sebastian Bachs," in *Mozart in Kursachsen* (Leipzig: Stadtgeschichtliches Museum Leipzig, 1991), 50–62.

6. "Erinnerung an Mozarts Aufenthalt zu Leipzig," *Berlinische musikalische Zeitung* 1 (1805): 132: "Am 22. April ließ er [Mozart] sich ohne vorausgehende Ankündigung und unentgeldlich auf der Orgel in der Thomaskirche hören. Er spielte da eine Stunde lang schön und kunstreich vor vielen Zuhörern. Der damalige Organist Görner und der verstorbene Cantor Doles waren neben ihm, und zogen die Register. Ich sah ihn selbst, einen jungen modisch gekleideten Mann, von Mittelgröße. Doles war

to do so and, as he emphasized in his letter, "not for lack of health and strength or of good will but rather because of certain manifold and important hindrances that he had encountered sometimes more often, sometimes less often" in his thirty-three-year cantorate. Even so, it gave him satisfaction to see that "a great number" of his former students "were in public offices." Moreover, he was only willing to step down if as emeritus he were allowed a substantial part of his salary and a rent-free apartment.[7] The town council immediately and generously accepted the conditions proposed by Doles. On 28 March 1789, Johann Adam Hiller was unanimously elected to be the new Thomaskantor. There is no record of any applicants other than Hiller, who was exempted from having to audition because, according to Mayor Müller, his "services to music" were "well known."[8]

However, it was only on 22 June—three months later—that Hiller signed his employment contract as new Thomaskantor. Six days later, on the third Sunday after Trinity, the seventy-five-year-old Cantor Doles conducted his farewell cantata *Ich komme vor dein Angesicht* and sang the part of the tenor soloist, as attested by a witness: "with his ageless and firm voice . . . that brought the large congregation to tears."[9] In 1790 Doles published his farewell cantata, which was dedicated to Johann Gottlieb Naumann and Mozart.[10] (See figure 6.2.)

In other words, Mozart's visit took place in between two cantorates. Doles, very frustrated about the way the Leipzig authorities dealt with him, had officially resigned in March, and was to be replaced by the young Hiller more or less against his will; but in May Hiller was not yet installed and still out of town. The fact that Mozart was in town and ready to play the organ in St. Thomas gave Doles a welcome opportunity to

---

ganz entzückt über des Künstlers Spiel, und glaubte den alten Seb. Bach (seinen Lehrer), für welchen Mozart auch auf der Thomasschule bei dem Anhören einer seiner Motetten und bei dem Anblick seiner Werke die innigste Verehrung ausdrückte, wieder auferstanden. Mozart hatte mit sehr gutem Anstande, und mit der größten Leichtigkeit alle harmonischen Künste angebracht, und die Themate, unter andern den Choral Jesu meine Zuversicht aufs Herrlichste aus dem Stegereife durchgeführt."

7. Doles's letter is published in ThomDOK 2, X/B 28: "daß ich, ohngeachtet der vielen und wichtigen Hinderniße, die ich bis itzt bald öfterer bald seltener auf meinem Wege fand, dennoch stets die von Gott mir verliehenen Kräffte und Kenntniße nach Möglichkeit zum Besten [. . .] anzuwenden mich bemühte [. . .] Umstände, [. . .] unter denen jedoch weder Mangel der Gesundheit und Kräfte noch des guten Willens sich befinden [. . .] mich [. . .] veranlasst haben."

8. Müller's remarks, which are part of the minutes of the town council meeting on the occasion of Hiller's election on 28 March 1789, are published in ThomDOK 2, XI/A 3.

9. See Michael Maul, *Bach's Famous Choir: The Saint Thomas School in Leipzig, 1212–1804* (Woodbridge, UK: Boydell Press, 2018), 258–61.

10. Maul, *Bach's Famous Choir*, 242.

Kantate

über das Lied des seel. Gellert:

Ich komme vor dein Angesicht u. s. w.

für

2 Hörner, 2 Hoboen, 1 Klarinette, 1 Fagott, 2 Violinen, 1 Bratsche,
4 Singestimmen, Instrumentalbässe, Orgel und Klavierauszug

verfertiget

und

zween seiner würdigsten Gönner und Freunde

Herrn Mozart

Kaiserlichem Kapellmeister in Wien

und

Herrn Naumann

Churfürstlich = Sächsischem Ober=Kapellmeister in Dreßden

aus vorzüglicher Hochachtung

zugeeignet

von

Johann Friedrich Doles

Kantor und Musikdirektor an den beiden Hauptkirchen zu Leipzig.

Leipzig,
gedruckt auf Kosten des Autors bei Christian Gottlob Täubel. 1790.

Figure 6.2. Title page of J. F. Doles, *Ich komme vor dein Angesicht* (Leipzig, 1790),
dedicated to Wolfgang Amadeus Mozart and Johann Gottlieb Naumann.
Courtesy of the Städtische Bibliotheken Leipzig-Musikbibliothek.

demonstrate his own musical legacy: the Thomaschor. Taking into account all those bad reviews he had received from the Leipzig authorities and his own school rector over the last years, Doles must have felt a real vindication in Mozart's praise of the quality of the choir and (from his perspective) a strong rebuke to his enemies on the town council.

Rochlitz said in his report that, at the instigation of Doles, the choir of the Thomasschule surprised Mozart with the performance of the double-choir motet "Singet dem Herrn ein neues Lied" (BWV 225). Rochlitz does not say that Doles conducted the performance himself, but this is not a surprise, since rehearsing and conducting the motets in the services was traditionally part of the prefect's duties. According to a handwritten notice concerning the life of Johann Friedrich Suckow, later financial councilor in Sonderhausen, in 1789 Suckow was prefect of the choir and, as the oldest among the boarders, conducted the performance in Mozart's presence.[11]

However, this information is doubtful for several reasons. First of all, according to the recently rediscovered school register book, Suckow enrolled at the Thomasschule only in May 1787 in the age of eighteen, and he left school five years later, in May 1792.[12] A printed obituary for Suckow, published in *Neuer Nekrolog der Deutschen* in 1842, includes information on his time at the school:

> At the Thomasschule in Leipzig, where he made significant progress, especially in the training of his musical skills and knowledge, first while studying with Cantor and Music Director Doles, then with Kapellmeister and Cantor Hiller, [Suckow] was proud to have been a Thomaner ... and he was allowed to show this pride in his modest and witty manner; for during his last three years at the school he administered the prefecture of the choirs. Finally, in his last year, he served as the general prefect and Hiller's deputy.[13]

In other words, as was common practice, Suckow apparently started his career as prefect in summer 1789, first serving as the prefect of the fourth choir and, after leading the third and second choirs, he became first or general prefect [*Generalpräfekt*] in 1791.

---

11. Schulze, "Mozarts Begegnung mit dem Leipziger Thomanerchor," 56.

12. The Thomasschule's register of matriculations ("Album Alumnorum Thomanorum"), 1730–1800, in Stadtarchiv Leipzig, Thomasschule Leipzig, No. 483:214v.

13. *Neuer Nekrolog der Deutschen* (1842): 14–15: "auf die Thomasschule zu Leipzig [...], auf der er [...] insbesondere in der Ausbildung seiner musikalischen Kenntnisse und Fertigkeiten, [...] zuerst unter dem Kantor und Musikdirektor Doles, dann unter dem Kapellmeister und Kantor Hiller bedeutende Fortschritte machte. [...] S. war stolz darauf, ein Thomaner [...] gewesen zu seyn und er durfte diesen Stolz in seiner anspruchslosen, launigen Weise zeigen; denn er hatte in den letzten 3 Jahren seines Besuches der Thomasschule die Präfektur der Chöre, in dem letzten Jahre vor seinem Abgang als Generalpräfektus und Hillers Amanuensis verwaltet."

The information given in Suckow's obituary is fully confirmed by the account books of the first choir, which I discovered several years ago.[14] These materials provide precise information concerning the constitution of the choirs and the names of the prefects. Here, starting in January 1789, Suckow signed as a member of the first choir and called himself "Prefect adjunctus"—which meant assistant to the prefect. Later that year he became prefect of the fourth choir, 1790 of the third, 1791 for a short period of the second choir, and finally prefect of the first choir.

The account books also reveal the name of the actual first or general prefect in spring 1789. It was the twenty-two-year-old Johann Friedrich Samuel Döring, who was at this time the oldest of the Thomaner. (See figure 6.3.) Born in 1766 in Gatterstädt, Thuringia, he enrolled at the Thomasschule in 1781 and left the school on 30 April 1789, just nine days after Mozart visited the school. Döring undertook his studies at Leipzig University.[15] In 1794 he was promoted to cantor in Luckau, Niederlausitz, one year later cantor in Görlitz, and finally in 1814 cantor in Altenburg, where he died in 1840.[16] When August Eberhard Müller resigned in 1809 from the St. Thomas cantorate, Döring was among the applicants for the position, however unsuccessful.[17]

Döring must have played a very prominent role in the choir during the last years of Doles's cantorate. When he applied for the Luckau cantorate in 1794 his teacher Doles wrote a warm letter of recommendation, praising Döring's musical skills to the skies.

> During the entire time of his tenure here at the Thomasschule and at Leipzig University, I had the uninterrupted opportunity to experience his aptitude in literature and his innate drive for vocal and instrumental music. His tireless diligence in literature and music earned him the affection of all of his teachers, and because he had a durable and pleasant bass voice, he always had the good fortune to serve as a concertist within the musical choir and afterward received all the prefectures one after another until the end of each school year.[18]

---

14. Account books ("Rationes Pecuniae Musicae") in Stadtarchiv Leipzig, Thomasschule Leipzig, No. 283. See also Michael Maul, "'Welche ieder Zeit aus den 8 besten Subjectis bestehen muß'—Die erste 'Cantorey' der Thomasschule: Organisation, Aufgaben, Fragen," *BJ* 99 (2013): 11–77, esp. 20–21.

15. The Thomasschule's register of matriculations ("Album Alumnorum Thomanorum"), 1730–1800, 201v, n. 8.

16. See Maul, "Die erste 'Cantorey' der Thomasschule," 36n10.

17. See ThomDOK, XII/A 8–9.

18. Quoted in ThomDOK, X/C 81: "weil ich die ganze Zeit seiner allhier auf der Thomasschule zugebrachten Schul- und Universitätsjahre ununterbrochene Gelegenheit gehabt habe, sein gutes Genie zur Litteratur und angebohrnen Trieb zur Vokal- und Instrumentalmusik, nicht weniger eine gute Anlage zur Setzkunst bei ihm wahrzunehmen. Sein unermüdeter Fleis in litteris und musicis erwarb ihm die Liebe aller seiner Lehrer, und wegen seiner dauerhaften und angenehmen Baßstimme war er

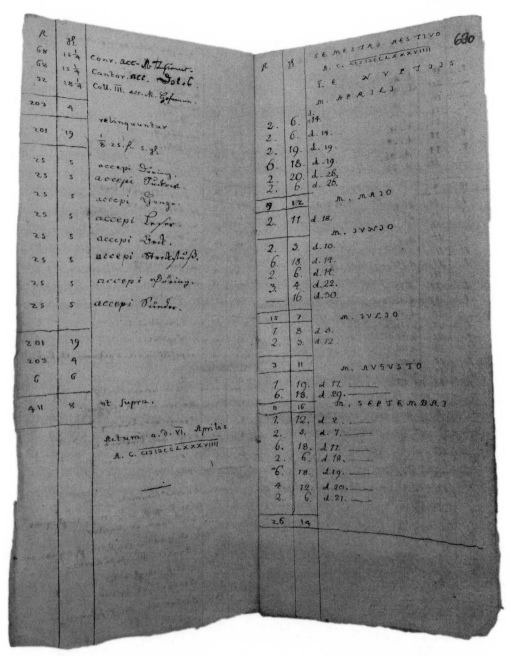

Figure 6.3. Account book of the "Pecuniae Musicae" with signatures of all of the members of the first Cantorey, with Johann Friedrich Samuel Döring on the top, dated 6 April 1789. Courtesy of the Stadtarchiv Leipzig.

Seeking further clues about Döring, I came across an obituary of him, also published in the *Nekrolog der Deutschen* after he died in 1840. Here one can find not only a reference to his years at the Thomasschule, but also to a personal encounter with Mozart.

In 1776, his beautiful soprano voice brought him to the Thomasschule in Leipzig as a boarder. Here, in addition to his scholarship, he educated himself in the arts to such an extent that after some years he became prefect of the choir. As such he made the personal acquaintance of Mozart, who was inclined to take him to Vienna. However, the young man preferred to continue his studies in Leipzig, where he was enrolled as a student of theology in 1789. After passing his candidate examination in Dresden in 1791, he served as a private tutor in a prestigious family, but had to give up the position the following year due to illness. In 1793 he became cantor in the town church of Luckau in Lower Lusatia.[19]

No doubt, the encounter with Mozart during Döring's time as prefect of the choir must refer to Mozart's visit to the school in April 1789, and taking into account that Döring at this time was not only the oldest Thomaner, but also the general prefect of the choir, there can be no doubt that he conducted the performance of the Bach motet. Obviously, according to the words in the obituary, which were surely based on information from the deceased himself, Döring impressed Mozart. Mozart's enthusiasm was probably related more to his qualities as a bass singer than as a leader of the choir; Mozart probably didn't have any need for choir conductors in Vienna, but he might have been on the lookout for good singers. Unfortunately, Döring's name does not appear in the pertinent Mozart documents; thus we can only speculate what Mozart actually had in mind when making Döring an offer. In any case, this offer obviously was not concrete or convincing enough to cause Döring to change his future plans. According to an entry in the school's register of matriculations, only ten days later Döring left the Thomasschule for Leipzig University.

---

immer so glücklich, im musikalischen Chore eine Konzertistenstelle und dann auch die Praefecturen nacheinander bis zum Ende der Schuljahre zu erhalten." On the relationship between Doles and Döring, see also ThomDOK, X/E 2.

19. *Neuer Nekrolog der Deutschen* (1840): 919: "Im Jahre 1776 brachte ihn sein schöner Sopran als Alumnus auf die Thomasschule in Leipzig. Hier bildete sich der Knabe neben seinen wissenschaftlichen Studien in der Kunst dergestalt, daß er nach einigen Jahren Chorpräfekt wurde. Als solcher machte er die persönliche Bekanntschaft Mozart's, der ihn mit nach Wien zu nehmen geneigt war. Der Jüngling zog es jedoch vor, seine Studien in Leipzig fortzusetzen, wo er sich 1788 [recte: 1789] als Student der Theologie inskribieren ließ. Nachdem er 1791 zu Dresden sein Kandidatenexamen bestanden hatte, wurde er Hauslehrer in einer angesehenen Familie, mußte aber diese Stellung Krankheitshalber im folgenden Jahre aufgeben. 1793 wurde er als Kantor in der Stadtkirche nach Lucka[u] in der Niederlausitz berufen."

Döring's obituary, however, provides good reason also to connect Döring—who was a brilliant bass singer according to Doles—with the aforementioned anecdote. Recall that Rochlitz, when citing Mozart's famous phrase on the outstanding quality of the choir, mentioned: "Among the crowd of at least forty singers he was particularly impressed by a certain bass singer. He started a short conversation with him and, without any of us present noticing anything, he pressed a handsome present into the young man's hand."

Therefore, this bass singer must have been Döring, and there is also good reason to believe that not only the little anecdote published by Rochlitz but also his famous longer report on Mozart's visit to the Thomasschule were both based to a certain extent on information he received from Döring, since they shared a long history together: Both enrolled as boarders at the Thomasschule in 1781, and both were invariably members of the first cantorey, those eight privileged singers who sang under the direction of Doles on all occasions when the choir performed for cash. Rochlitz, however, left school in April 1788; therefore in all likelihood he wasn't an eyewitness to Mozart's visit in April 1789 and must have received the relevant information from some of his former schoolmates.

In case Döring actually did serve as one of his informants, it would be understandable why he also knew about the fact that Mozart surprised that particular bass singer with a precious gift, given in a way that nobody else noticed.

Taking a closer look into Döring's later life and his multifaceted activities not only as composer but also as an author of musical treatise, we find some references that confirm his particular interest and intense adoration of Bach's music, especially of Bach's motets. Starting in 1796 he published more or less on a regular basis a series of official school lectures, given while cantor in the city of Görlitz. They are titled *Etwas zur Berichtigung des Urtheils über die musikalischen Singechöre auf den gelehrten protestantischen Schulen Deutschlands* (Something to correct the general opinion on musical choirs in German Protestant schools). In the 1806 volume he talked about proper conditions and environment for a school choir. In this context he emphasized that it would be important that

the arias and motets are not merely rehearsed and sung from the performing parts, but that each individual student can read and carefully study the scores, as well as the piano scores of larger works. Hiller's printed motets, the eight-voice motets by Bach, Haydn's *Creation* and *Seasons* in excerpts, etc. should therefore not be missing in any collection. And without grandstanding as a judge, I would like to add that in my eyes, a choir that is only able to perform motets by [Johann Gottfried] Weiske, Doles, etc., ranks only among the middle level. However, where [Ernst Wilhelm] Wolf, [Carl Heinrich] Graun, [Gottfried August] Homilius, and Sebastian Bach reign, there the highest standard has been achieved! . . . The boys of our Görlitz School Choir have subsequently acquired Bach's motets at their own expense. Meanwhile they have studied these pieces to the benefit of their intellectual skills and they are performing these pieces on a level that exceeds even the quality of Thomaner in Leipzig during the years 1784–88.[20]

In the Görlitz municipal library I came across a manuscript by Döring, in which he described an educational trip to Berlin he made in 1804. After visiting the king's opera house he also attended a rehearsal of the Berlin Singakademie. Fully convinced and overwhelmed by the quality of the institution and the way Carl Friedrich Zelter conducted the choir, Döring wrote:

Anyone who has not heard the entire coetus of the Thomaner in Leipzig singing an eight-voice motet can have no idea of the effect of pure singing voices. But even this choir lacks the knowledge of the very special Zelter manner . . . Vocal-Symphony could approximately express what the man has invented. The pieces his choir used to sing are not only for the church, like those of Bach and the eight-part motets by Harrer and Doles, but for the pure entertainment of the society itself. . . . If someone who understands the matter demands of me an even clearer and more specific proof of the quality of each individual singer, then I can assure them, even without having attended all of the rehearsals, that I have not heard a single impure tone and have noticed the wobbling in intonation only once. Thus, every member must be steady in keeping time and in tune before being accepted into society. . . . I cannot claim that I ever heard a choir pronouncing the words better, or at least more evenly. Unfortunately, Meisseners call it affected if a single person pronounces "spricht" instead of the rather rude "schpricht" [with a strong Saxon accent], and we are wrong in doing so. Oh well, this was a pure joy to my ears![21]

20. Johann Friedrich Samuel Döring, *Etwas zur Berichtigung des Urtheils über die musikalischen Singechöre auf den gelehrten protestantischen Schulen Deutschlands* (Görlitz, 1806), 17: "Daß die Arien und Motetten nicht etwa bloß aus den Stimmen einstudirt und gesungen werden, sondern, daß jeder einzelne Schüler die Partituren davon, so wie Klavierauszüge größerer Musiken lesen und studiren könne. Hillers gesammelte Motetten, die achtstimmigen Bachischen, Haydns Schöpfung und die Jahreszeiten im Auszuge etc. sollten daher nirgends fehlen. [. . .] Ohne mich übrigens als Taxator aufdringen zu wollen, setze ich noch hinzu, daß in meinen Augen ein Chor, welches bloß Motetten von Weißke, Doles etc. vorzutragen im Stande ist, doch nur unter die mittleren gehört, wo hingegen Wolf, Graun, Homilius und S. Bach regieren, da, da ist das höchste und letzte in dieser Art! [. . .] die Mitglieder desselben [Görlitzer Singechors] [. . .] haben [. . .] sich in der Folge die achtstimmigen Motetten von Bach selbst angeschafft, und sie nun bereits auch alle, zu ihrem großen, versteht sich aber bloß intellektuellen Vortheile so produzirt [. . .], als es in den Jahren 1784–88 die Thomasschüler in Leipzig nicht konnten."

21. Oberlausitzische Bibliothek der Wissenschaften Göritz, Archiv OLGdW, VIII 24: "Einige Bemerkungen über Musik, gemacht auf einer Reise nach Berlin u. vorgelesen in der Lausitzischen Gesellschaft der Wissenschaften, den 25. April, 1804." "Wer nicht wenigstens einmal den ganzen

Döring's obvious enthusiasm for the motets of Bach is documented in the fact that it was he who published with Breitkopf in 1819 the first edition of the famous motet "Jauchzet dem Herrn" (BWV Anh. 160), attributed to both Bach and Georg Philipp Telemann. (See figure 6.4.) In the preface Döring pointed out, regarding the third movement of the piece: "The following was given as Telemann's work in the oldest performing parts in the Thomasschule, which were still undamaged in 1789. But Johann Friedrich Doles and David Traugott Nicolai assured that it was an addition by [Gottlob] Harrer, Bach's successor in office."[22]

A manuscript of this piece and a copy of Bach's motet "Singet dem Herrn" (BWV 225) are preserved in the music collection of Gesellschaft der Musikfreunde in Vienna as part of Mozart's estate. Both are written on Saxon paper by the same copyist. They are considered the copies Mozart received after visiting the Thomasschule.[23] The obvious assumption that Döring might have been the anonymous copyist of both scores is not confirmed by a comparison of handwriting. However, what I noticed are several similarities between the anonymous copyist of the two Viennese manuscripts with the handwriting of Friedrich Wilhelm Leser, in 1789 a member of the first cantorey of the Thomaner, but I need to examine more documents in Leser's hand to reach a final conclusion.

Coetus der Thomasschüler in Leipzig eine 8stimmige Motette hat singen hören, kan sich gar keine Vorstellung von der Wirkung blosser Singestimmen machen. Aber auch diesem fehlt noch die Kenntniß der ganz eigenen Zelterischen Manier. [. . .] Vocal-Symphonie könnte ohngefähr ausdrücken, was der Mann erfunden hat. Die Sachen selbst sind nicht bloß für die Kirche, wie die Bachischen u. die 8stimmigen Motetten von Harrer u. Doles, sondern für die bloße Unterhaltung dieser Gesellschaft selbst. [. . .] Fordert mir jemand, der die Sache verstehet, einen noch deutlichern u. specielleren Beweis der Güte jedes einzelnen Individuums ab, so kann ich auch da, ohne gerade alle Proben gehört zu haben, geradezu versichern, daß ich auch nicht einen unreinen Ton gehört u. das Wancken in der Bewegung nur ein einzigmal bemerkt habe. Tact u. Tonfest muß also jedes Mitglied schon vor der Aufnahme in die Gesellschaft seyn. [. . .] Die Aussprache noch zu erwähnen, kan ich mich nicht rühmen, ja ein auch viel kleineres Chor besser wenigstens egaler aussprechen gehört zu haben. Wir Meißner nennen es z.B. affectirt, wenn ein einzelner statt des derben schpricht, lieber spricht; u. wir thun Unrecht. Wie wohl that doch gerade dieß [. . .] meinen Ohren!"

22. *"Jauchzet dem Herrn," alle Welt c. c. Achtstimmige Motette von Johann Sebastian Bach in Partitur. Herausgegeben von Joh. Fr. Sam. Doering* (Leipzig: Ch. E. Kollmann: [1819]): "Das folgende wurde in den ältesten Stimmen der Thomasschule, welche 1789 noch unbeschädigt waren, als Telemanns Arbeit angegeben. Joh. Fr. Doles und Dav. Traug. Nicolai versicherten aber: es sey ein additamentum von Harrer, dem Nachfolger Bachs im Amte." See also NBA III/3, KB, 40–41. Nicolai was a student at Leipzig University 1753–55, from 1758 till his death in 1799 organist in Görlitz, where Döring served as cantor from 1795 onward.

23. A-Wgm, A 169b and V 6090 (H 29572). See Christine Blanken, *Die Bach-Quellen in Wien und Alt-Österreich—Katalog*, 2 vols. (Hildesheim: Olms, 2011): 1:178–79, 207.

Figure 6.4. Title page of the motet "Jauchzet den Herrn" (BWV Anh. 160).
Courtesy of the Bach-Archiv Leipzig.

My careful examination of the documents concerning Mozart's visit reveals that the prefect Döring obviously played an important role not only in this particular performance of a Bach motet, but also as one of those figures who paved the way for a broader Bach renaissance at the turn of nineteenth century.

Even if we tend to take it for granted that Bach's motets over the course of the second half of eighteenth century were part of the main and permanent repertoire of the choir, one could ask: Was this also the case under Doles's cantorate, as implied by statements by Gerber and Rochlitz that are not entirely clear in their interpretation? Or is this common point of view influenced by the story about Mozart's visit to the school?[24] The fact that Döring later considered the motets by Doles of only middling quality and clearly preferred Bach's motets raises the question whether it was mainly a decision by the prefect that the choir surprised Mozart with a piece by the former cantor Bach and not with a composition by the cantor emeritus Doles. In any case, we should not underestimate the impact this wonderful story obviously had on the rediscovery of Bach's motets and to the fact that in 1803 Breitkopf published the first edition of these outstanding pieces. At least, the story that the divine genius Mozart literally fell on his knees while listening to this music laid the perfect ground for this story of success and for the still ongoing tradition to please important guests at the Thomasschule with a performance of a Bach motet.

24. Concerning this ongoing discussion, based not least by the question of the right interpretation of remarks by Ernst Ludwig Gerber, in the article on J. S. Bach in *Neues historisch-biographisches Lexikon der Tonkünstler* (Leipzig, 1812), 1:222–23, and *Rochlitz in Für Freunde der Tonkunst* (Leipzig, 1830), 2:211–12, see Hans-Joachim Schulze, *Studien zur Bach-Überlieferung im 18. Jahrhundert* (Leipzig: Peters, 1984), 94; Andreas Glöckner, "Bach-Aufführungen unter Johann Friedrich Doles," *Händel-Jahrbuch* 40 (2001): 245–47; and Uwe Wolf, "Zur Leipziger Aufführungstradition der Motetten Bachs im 18. Jahrhundert," *BJ* 91 (2005): 301–9 (esp. 303–6).

CONTRIBUTORS

PAUL CORNEILSON is managing editor of *Carl Philipp Emanuel Bach: The Complete Works* at the Packard Humanities Institute and the author of *The Autobiography of Ludwig Fischer: Mozart's First Osmin*.

YOEL GREENBERG is senior lecturer and head of the music department at Bar-Ilan University.

NOELLE M. HEBER is a violinist, musicologist, and educator based in Berlin.

MICHAEL MAUL is head of research at the Bach-Archiv Leipzig and intendant of the Bachfest.

STEPHEN ROE is a music antiquarian and writer in London.

DAVID SCHULENBERG is a professor of music at Wagner College, New York, and a performer on early keyboard instruments.

ELEANOR SELFRIDGE-FIELD is an adjunct professor of music at Stanford University and managing director of the Center for Computer-Assisted Research in the Humanities, an affiliate of the Packard Humanities Institute.

GENERAL INDEX

INDEX OF WORKS

Bach Perspectives
is a publication of the
American Bach Society,
dedicated to promoting the study
and performance of the music of
Johann Sebastian Bach.
Membership information is available online at
www.americanbachsociety.org.

THE BACH PERSPECTIVES SERIES

The University of Illinois Press
is a founding member of the
Association of University Presses.

———————————————

Composed in 10/14 Janson Text
by Jim Proefrock
at the University of Illinois Press
Manufactured by Sheridan Books, Inc.

University of Illinois Press
1325 South Oak Street
Champaign, IL 61820-6903
www.press.uillinois.edu